Simon Garfield is the author of, amongst others, *The End of Innocence: Britain in the Time of AIDS* (winner of the Somerset Maugham Award), *The Wrestling*, *The Nation's Favourite: The True Adventures of Radio 1* and *Mauve*, which was hailed in the *Daily Telegraph* as 'a book about science which also happens to be a miniature work of art.' *The Last Journey of William Huskisson* was a book of the week on BBC Radio 4.

'A brightly polished and well turned modern "penny-dreadful", an illustrated melodrama that brings to life the opening of the Liverpool and Manchester Railway on September 15, 1830.' Jonathan Glancey, *Guardian*

'A horrible death, which Garfield records with the quality of forensic detail which animates the whole of this book . . . The dawn of the railways was marked by greed, for sure. But also by a marvellous optimism and swash-buckling energy, which shines throughout this book.' *Independent on Sunday*

'The event of his death is used here only as a backdrop for a much wider picture. What unfolds is an engaging look at the political climate of Britain on the brink of empire and industrial might, with the railways as one of the most vital tools for implementing this. This book should appeal to more than just the train spotter that Huskisson most certainly wasn't.' *New Statesman*

'Garfield has written an instant winner of a yarn, he steams ahead like Stephenson's Rocket. Into the account of the fatal day, he weaves a whole network of connecting themes: civil unrest, politics, trade, economics – and optical illusions.' Jonathan Sale, *Independent*

'Garfield's story is at once a history of the railway as well as an account of Huskisson's eventful life . . . by linking the conflict between progress and reaction to the tussle between Huskisson's liberal leanings and the ultra-Conservatism of Wellington's government, Garfield has created a vibrant picture of the time.' *The Times*

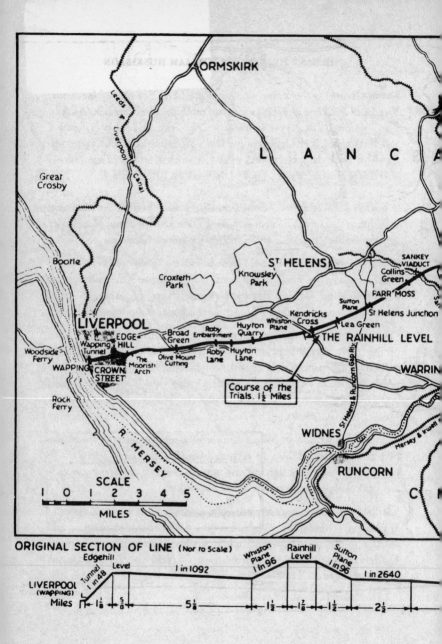

ORMSKIRK

L A N C A

Great
Crosby

Leeds & Liverpool Canal

Bootle

St HELENS

SANKEY
VIADUCT

Collins
Green

FARR' MOSS

Croxteth
Park

Knowsley
Park

Sutton
Plane

St Helens Junction

LIVERPOOL

Woodside
Ferry

EDGE-
HILL

Wapping
Tunnel

WAPPING

CROWN
STREET

The
Moorish
Arch

Rock
Ferry

Broad
Green

Roby
Embankment

Olive Mount
Cutting

Roby
Lane

Huyton
Quarry

Huyton
Lane

Whiston
Plane

Kendricks
Cross

Lea Green

THE RAINHILL LEVEL

St Helens & Runcorn Gap Rly.

WARRIN

Course of the
Trials. 1½ Miles

WIDNES

RUNCORN

Mersey & Irwell

C

R. MERSEY

SCALE

```
1  0  1  2  3  4  5
```

MILES

ORIGINAL SECTION OF LINE (Not to Scale)

Edgehill

Level

Whiston Plane
1 in 96

Rainhill
Level

Sutton
Plane
1 in 96

Tunnel
1 in 48

1 in 1092

1 in 2640

LIVERPOOL
(WAPPING)

Miles

1⅛

5/0

5⅛

1½

1⅞

1½

2½

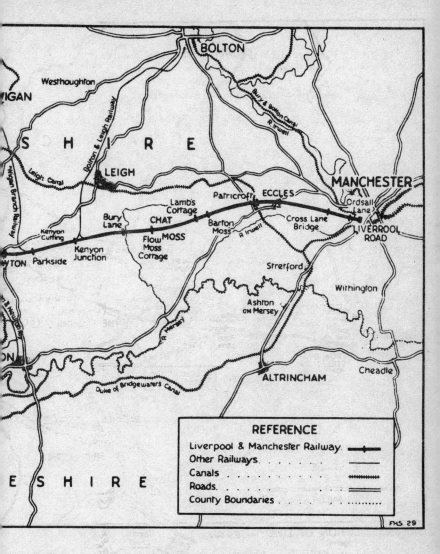

WIGAN

Westhoughton

BOLTON

- S - H - I - R - E

Bolton & Leigh Railway

Bury & Bolton Canal

R. Irwell

Leigh Canal

LEIGH

Kenyon Branch Railway

Lamb's Cottage

Parricroft

ECCLES

MANCHESTER

Ordsall Lane

Bury Lane

CHAT

Barton Moss

Cross Lane Bridge

LIVERPOOL ROAD

Kenyon Cutting

Flow Moss Cottage

MOSS

Moss Cottage

R. Irwell

WYTON

Parkside

Kenyon Junction

Strerford

Withington

R. Mersey

Ashton on Mersey

TON

Duke of Bridgewaters Canal

ALTRINCHAM

Cheadle

- E - S - H - I - R - E

REFERENCE

Liverpool & Manchester Railway	—•—•—
Other Railways	————
Canals	++++++
Roads	════
County Boundaries	··········

FHS 29

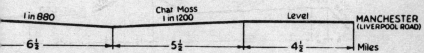

1 in 880

Chat Moss
1 in 1200

Level

MANCHESTER
(LIVERPOOL ROAD)

6½ — 5½ — 4½ — Miles

THE LAST JOURNEY OF
WILLIAM HUSKISSON

Simon Garfield

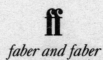

faber and faber

First published in 2002
by Faber and Faber Limited
3 Queen Square London WC1N 3AU
This paperback first published in 2003

Typeset by Faber and Faber Ltd in Bulmer
Printed in England by Mackays of Chatham plc

A CIP record for this book
is available from the British Library

ISBN 0–571–21608–0

2 4 6 8 10 9 7 5 3 1

To the memory of my mother and father

There were a great many witnesses to the terrible accident which befell William Huskisson, but none could agree precisely what occurred. Some said his left leg fell on the track in one way, some quite another, and some said it was his thigh. A few observed a 'fiery fountain' of blood, but others saw only a trickle. Some claimed there was shrieking, but the rest believed he was rendered mute by the shock. Yet there was one thing on which everyone agreed. They all said that the accident was the worst thing they had ever seen, and the one thing they would never forget.

The following pages recount how a day of triumph became a day of despair at the turn of a wheel.

Contents

PART ONE

A New Impulse

The opening: ancient notions overthrown in a day.

AT PARKSIDE WATER STOP, near Newton, at a little after five on the morning of 15 September 1830, more than seven hours before the accident, a group of grey-skinned men could be seen working on the brand new railway, sweeping the tarnished line that would stretch from Liverpool to Australia. A stray chipping or clump or earth might throw the engines clean from the track, and they had been out for hours clearing the way with brushes made from oak twigs, scratching and polishing the iron route in one action, checking for bad links and broken joints. Sixty men in all, each assigned half a mile and the promise of generous payment. It was an honour, they were told, but it was also a dangerous and very modern pursuit.

It was raining, but clearing. The dawn would bring fresh winds, the same gusts that would wake residents at the Adelphi Hotel, alarming them with the terror that they had missed the very thing they had travelled to Liverpool to witness. Some held their tickets in their palms as they slept, and their doors were locked against intruders.

The men on the tracks wore sodden worsted jackets, but the wind blew through every fibre, and soon their faces would be bluish-red. As they brushed, more grit swept in behind them, so as to make their task a hopeless one. This was the last job on the railway – truly the last – and when they stepped aside, the engines would hurry past them in a whorl of delight, the hot clank of cast iron and burning steam, a smith's forge in brutal motion through a startled landscape. There used to be livestock along this line, but now even birds won't take a look.

There were men brushing by every bridge, and as the light improved they could see the next bridge and the one beyond, some still wet not from rain but from building, the ooze of muggy sand seeping beneath their curved brick slabs. These men had built the bridges and laid the rails, and cast the blocks and sleepers on which they ran, and their recent lives could be measured on each section of the track. They had been threatened and stoned at every mile from Wapping to Salford, but now it was over. On this day there were no sections any more, but a streaming, knotty line slipped between two towns like a vein in a grey mare's neck.

The men lived in fear of attack, and of accident. Since the earliest surveys, they had suffered unholy deaths, disasters of the sort that had never been heard of before. They spoke of a man named John Kent, shoring up a heavy load of clay at Edge Hill, 'fourteen or fifteen feet high, when the mass fell upon him, and literally crushed his bowels out of his body.' It was said they could lay almost the entire line on sleepers made from injured men's legs.

Near St Helens, another melancholy occurrence: George Cockscroft was walking by the side of a horse drawing wagons, when his foot slipped and he fell. A newspaper told how 'his legs were unfortunately across the rail, when several wagon wheels passed over them, and crushed them so severely that both were obliged to be amputated.' He lingered in great pain until the next evening, when he died at eight o'clock. He left a wife and five children, whom he had hardly seen in a year on account of his ceaseless attempt to get the railway open as scheduled and render it safe.

THAT NIGHT, Henry Booth slept with a gun by his bedside. He had reason for apprehension. Booth was the official secretary and treasurer to the Liverpool and Manchester Railway Company, its chief protector and proselytiser, and he had designed

4

the little things that would make it work – the clever carriage couplings, the special boiler. He was not yet recognised for his deeds, and in the place of acclaim he found mainly the stern countenance of his investors. It was worth considering what could go wrong: there may be explosions and locomotives leaping the tracks into thundering crowds; there may be delays and slow speeds, perhaps nervous dogs, infirm passengers, a leakage of tanks. None of this would happen, he hoped, because none of this had happened on the test runs, and he was a religious man with a faith in fair Providence.

It was about 5.45 a.m. Even sheeted in his Liverpool bed he appeared a slight and bookish man, his face craggy but timid. In his early life he was as interested in poetry as in mechanics, and one of his first verses was called 'Commerce' (although he considered his best work to be 'Sebastian', a tragedy). He didn't look like a man who was going to be remembered.

As things turned out, he was to be remembered as a visionary. Booth was a multi-talented, highly opinionated man, a witty reformer of modern ills who spoke stubbornly against the Corn Laws and the Poor Law and the risks of overpopulation. He was a corn merchant, a civic politician and a man to be called on for the big odd jobs of the day – installing a heating system in a new church, improving the propulsion of canal boats, investing in the first steamship to carry passengers from Liverpool to Bagillt on the Dee in north Wales.

Some months before the opening of the railway, he had written of a place where 'the genius of the age, like a mighty river of the new world, flows onward, full, rapid, and irresistible', a peculiarly watery image for his plans for the permanent way of his railroad, but the sense was unerring, and it took a great deal of courage to write like that in those times. He went on: 'Notions which we have received from our ancestors, and verified by our own experience, are overthrown in a day, and a new standard erected, by which to form our ideas of the future.'

5

Booth faced ridicule and scorn for his belief in steam locomotion. Ordinary people would never step on the railroad. They thought a journey at speed would crush their lungs. The rumours that began in mischief came to be believed: the railway, violent over peaceful land, would turn a cow's milk sour. People bought his pamphlets not just for education but for lazy amusement. When Booth foresaw the extension of railways throughout the country, a hundred lines or more, they thought he had lost his sense of reason. The traveller would hence live a life twice as useful, he believed, for a journey of ten hours would now take five. 'The man of business in Manchester will breakfast at home,' Booth told nervous assemblies, 'proceed to Liverpool by the railway, transact his business, and return to Manchester before dinner.' A hard day's journeying would thus be converted into a morning's excursion.

The new age would begin in four hours. Booth lay in the last dawn where the weather, not the trains, alone rattled the urban windows and gave our brickwork its devilish shake. From this day on, the gun at his bedside would greet the railway by trembling to the edge of the table.

He would rise in an hour and make his way to the new station, where he believed he should be the first to arrive. But he would be mistaken, for many people were already walking towards the line, dressed as if for a carnival, unworried by the elements, their heads full of steam and sparks and the whiff of peril, and all curious to discover if the railroad would send them truly into the future – the iron and golden age in happy alchemy! – or whether it would melt itself down spectacularly before their eyes.

HOW WOULD the locomotives like the wet? The rain scoured the track like a wash of foundry filings, but the engines had been tested mainly in fine weather, and there had been talk of the wheels losing friction and slipping off the rails in a downpour.

The workmen looked up at the crowds converging to inspect their handiwork, and detected great local pride and great northern pride; this was not the first railway to be built, but it was undeniably the greatest. The railway builders – they were recently called 'navigators' and would soon be 'navvies' (from afar their digging resembled the ditching they had once performed for the canals) – had learnt that a few months before the opening of this line, the Canterbury and Whitstable Railway had rolled out its first passenger trucks, as if to spite their grander project. But those carriages were hauled by ropes attached to engines fixed to the ground and they only travelled a mile, and the Liverpool men liked to dismiss them as principally useful for the transportation of oysters.

The Liverpool–Manchester run was something entirely different. It was to be the fastest railway in the world and the first to link two large towns. It was the first extended railway with twin parallel tracks replacing the crude passing places on earlier lines. It was by far the most expensive and ambitious engineering project ever undertaken. It was the first to promise a gala opening combining royal coronation, public holiday, funfair, technological miracle and a journey conducted entirely by locomotive. It was a modern passenger railway, the longest piece of track the world had seen. Local people knew it was an event of the utmost significance, for it would draw the Prime Minister to the north of England.

The Liverpool and Manchester. The 'and' was the only acceptable usage, for 'to' caused civic jealousies and worked against the notion of two-way traffic; it wasn't like the earlier colliery trains returning empty to their filling stations. This line was the first to make grand claims of its own importance, and today it would stake a claim upon posterity with a celebrity parade.

WILLIAM HUSKISSON had been advised not to attend. The Member of Parliament for Liverpool had recently been diagnosed with strangury, a tender inflammation of the kidneys and bladder, lending him a constant but unfulfilled desire to pass water. He had first experienced these symptoms at the funeral of George IV at Windsor in July, when he was forced to seek shade and attention in St George's Chapel. His medical men ordered an operation, and it made him miss his re-election. One of his doctors was William George Maton, physician to Queen Charlotte and the young Princess Victoria, who told him to cancel all forthcoming engagements.

Huskisson was used to this. In truth, he had drifted into the arena of the unwell not long after his birth. As a child he was malnourished and frequently laid up with chest complaints. Once, rising from his bed to do schoolwork, he fractured his arm. His horse fell on him just before his marriage. He was flattened by the pole of a carriage at the entrance to Horse Guards. When once in Scotland at the residence of the Duke of Athol, he tried to leap the moat but missed, savagely spraining his ankle and lacerating the tendons of his foot, the wrench of both permanently altering his gait and ensuring it would be many weeks before he was able to travel back to England. A while later he fell from a horse, and again broke his arm. He snapped it again not long after, this time by falling from a carriage. 'I do not by any means', wrote his friend George Canning, 'like the accounts of the numbness in your arm,' and he was right to be concerned. It was a complex fracture, the forebone splitting its entire length, and though many physicians tried to mend it, Huskisson never fully recovered its use. In 1827, Huskisson received what he called a 'decided attack of inflammation of the trachea', a condition that rendered his voice permanently raspy. His recovery period in France did not begin well: at Calais he tripped on a cable and lacerated his foot.

William Huskisson, who ignored the advice of his physician.

The accidents were not confined to his side of the family. In the spring of 1799 Huskisson married Emily Milbanke, the youngest daughter of Admiral Mark Milbanke, a naval commander-in-chief at Portsmouth (and the brother of Ralph Milbanke, the grandfather of Anne Isabella, wife of Lord Byron). Not long after the ceremony, Admiral Milbanke, eighty-two, plummeted to an exciting and unexpected death by falling over the banisters at his house in Upper Wimpole Street and landing on the marble floor of his hall.

Understandably, Huskisson would have failed to detect any humour in this or his own disasters. He was not a particularly humorous man. He was forthright and ambitious, and a man

9

blessed with some vision. Above all he was an honourable MP, a great supporter of his local constituents in Liverpool. After his operation at the end of July 1830, Huskisson's medical team provided him with a certificate to ward off unwanted invitations: 'From the state of debility in which Mr Huskisson's illness has left him, we are of the opinion that it would be extremely hazardous for him to undertake a long journey or to incur any abnormal fatigue or exertion for some weeks.' Huskisson noted this advice, but shortly afterwards resolved to attend the opening of the railway, a feat he proclaimed the most impressive of his lifetime.

I N OCTOBER 1824, Henry Booth and Charles Lawrence, Liverpool's mayor, drew up a prospectus with the aims of attracting finance and parliamentary approval for what many considered the wildest of schemes. The text embraced themes of economy, convenience, expeditiousness. It tried to allay all doubts of the future. It punished the canals.

The route between Liverpool and Manchester by rail was to be thirty-three miles, seventeen less than the existing journey by water. Engineers had already been out for a year surveying the land, their chosen route dotting their maps like a pearl string, from the Prince's Dock to Vauxhall Road, to Bootle, to Walton, Fazakerley, Croxteth, Kirkby, Knowsley, Eccleston, Windle, Sutton, Haydock, Newton in Mackerfield, Golborn, Lowton, Leigh, Pennington, Astley, Irlam, Worsley, Eccles, Pendlebury, Salford, Hume, and into Manchester by way of Water Street. It was a well-plotted arc, disruptive to few, gentlest in gradient. The beauty of it made the engineers sigh.

But it would be dear. The total cost, including locomotives, was estimated at £400,000, to be raised by 4,000 shares of £100. The cost for freight would be 10 shillings per ton, compared to 15 shillings by canal. The journey, which by canal took thirty-six hours by a winding route in fine weather, was estimated at four or five rail hours in the worst conditions. But the estimates would be way out: over the next six years, the journey time would halve, and the costs would double. It rapidly became apparent that the promoters of the railway had great trouble keeping pace with their own creation. They had only the faintest notion of what they were building.

THE ADELPHI HOTEL had opened in 1826 on Copperas Hill, the northernmost house in a small row of properties built thirty years before. Its central location made it an immediate success, and the proprietor James Radley found little difficulty attracting the most notable visitors of his day.

Throughout August 1830 his clientele included several people who had travelled far to see the principal amusement at the Adelphi Theatre, an elephant able to kneel and trot on the simplest commands and to carry a glass bucket of water on the lip of his trunk without spilling.

On 6 September, Radley was upset to hear that the elephant had extended his repertoire. Two keepers travelled everywhere with this stupendous animal, but it appeared that one of them, Monsieur Baptist Bernard, had given it some offence. It was well known that these animals don't easily forgive a slight, and so it transpired for poor Bernard. With little warning, the elephant seized Bernard with his trunk. His cries of 'Murder!' went unheeded, and the elephant threw him on the ground and trampled him. The enraged animal then attacked Bernard's assistant, lacerating his leg.

With the elephant's engagement at the Adelphi Theatre cancelled, several rooms were suddenly freed up for the opening of the railroad. On the evening of 14 September two of these were occupied by the Kemble family, an acting troupe at the height of their powers. Charles Kemble had been a celebrated leading man for two decades (his sister was Sarah Siddons, the leading tragic heroine of her day) and was currently at the Theatre Royal as Beverly in *The Gamester* and Mercutio in *Romeo and Juliet*. But it was his twenty-one-year-old daughter Fanny who was all the rage. The year before, her performance of Juliet in Covent Garden had been the singular triumph of the London season, and she was now repeating the role to acclaim and full houses in Liverpool. 'Her balcony scene is rich in all the simple sweetness of a youthful heart,' the *Liverpool Times* noted. 'She soars at once to that eminence from whence she displays the high powers of her mind.' It appears that she occasionally immersed herself in her character to damaging degrees. Her father told a friend that after one performance he 'was obliged to carry her into her dressing-room, where she screamed for five minutes.'

On account of their fame, the Kembles had been offered three tickets to the opening on the 15th. 'People are bidding almost anything for a place,' Fanny told a friend. Fearing that she would be unable to attend, due to her father wishing to perform in Heidelberg, she accepted an invitation to a trial run. 'You cannot conceive what that sensation of cutting the air was,' she informed her confidante, Harriet St Leger. 'The motion is as smooth as possible . . . I could either have read or written; and as it was, I stood up, and with my bonnet up "drank the air before me".' The wind weighed her eyelids down. She likened the experience to standing behind Niagara Falls. 'When I closed my eyes this sensation of flying was quite delightful, and strange beyond description; yet, strange as it was, I had a perfect sense of security, and not the slightest fear.'

S HORTLY AFTER DAWN, which broke at a few moments after six, the men who had built the railway followed the sinuous trail to its start, although a few remained to wait for the safe passage of the trains. Boisterous crowds continued to gather behind the iron railings (newly erected to protect bystanders from the railway and to protect the railway from objectors). The men walked on with some disquiet; some complained that they had not themselves been asked to ride on the opening day. There was talk of further work on new lines and new canals, but it was far from certain which would provide the securest employment.

The idea of a railway was not new. Wooden rails had been in common use in Britain in the sixteenth century, and since the first horse-drawn colliery wagonway was introduced in the mines of Nottinghamshire, hundreds of crude lines were laid to take coal to the nearest waterways. Iron rails became widespread at the end of the eighteenth century and private companies applied horses to pull goods and passengers between towns such as Croydon and Wandsworth, in south London, and Swansea and Mumbles in Wales. By 1825, there had been at least twenty-two acts of parliament describing the larger of the railways linking colliery, foundry or factory to a waterway. But the men who built the Liverpool and Manchester Railway had an idea that their work was something more important than this.

On their way back, the workmen observed the assembly of decorated booths, from which they could buy trinkets – cups and tankards and trays – commemorating the day at prices they could hardly afford. Some stalls sold souvenir pamphlets, including one by Henry Booth and one by James Scott Walker, a former Liverpool merchant's clerk who had become excited by the potential of steam during his time as assistant editor of the *Liverpool Mercury* in the 1820s. Walker had befriended the principal founders of the railway, and his writing reflected their own enthusiasms in a style befitting the fairground barker. 'The husbandman, and the careful housewife, may leave their distant homes on the border of the line,' he proclaimed, 'with their several important articles of consumption, and speedily arrive at their respective marts, without enduring the protracted delay and jostling of a market cart, which tends to unhinge them for the day.'

Henry Booth had a keener eye for detail and figures, and demonstrated how the canals struggled to cope with the huge boom in trade between Liverpool and Manchester in the last decades. In 1760, the number of vessels that paid a dock duty at Liverpool was 2,560; by 1824, when the Railway Company had formed, it was 10,000; in 1829 it was 11,303. In 1784, when eight bags of cotton arrived in Liverpool from America, customs officials were persuaded to open a new ledger; in 1824 there were 409,670 bags; by 1829 the total importation was 640,998. Of all the cotton entering Britain, Liverpool handled four-fifths.

In 1760 the population of Liverpool was about 26,000, with 22,000 in Manchester. By 1824 the numbers were 135,000 and 150,000. The first steam engine was used in a Manchester factory in 1790 and by 1824 there were more than 200. In 1824 the quantity of all goods passing between Liverpool and Manchester each day was 1,000 tons, and by 1830 it was 1,300 tons.

Joseph Sandars, a Liverpool corn merchant and underwriter, had observed this growth for several years, and for a while was persuaded that the existing network of turnpikes and canals need merely improve their efficiency to handle the increased traffic. But between 1818 and 1821 he witnessed the opposite, as the transport owners increased their profits while operating at their sluggish leisure. There were three canal routes serving Liverpool and Manchester. The oldest, the Mersey and Irwell Navigation, began operating in the 1720s, and remained the only water link between the towns until the Duke of Bridgewater's Canal opened from Runcorn to Manchester in 1776. Forty-five years later a link from Wigan on the Leeds and Liverpool Canal provided a third route, and all three operated at immense benefit to their owners, who made fortunes from charging colossal passage and storage fees. 'Against the most arbitrary exactions the public have hitherto had no protection,' Henry Booth observed. 'And against the indefinite continuance or recurrence of the evil, they have but one security.' Their security was the coming of the railroad. As Booth and Charles Lawrence wrote in alarming capitals in a document of 1824, 'IT IS COMPETITION THAT IS WANTED'.

The turnpike road, though poorly maintained and unsuitable for heavy or larger loads, was the only viable choice for passenger traffic. By 1825, twenty-two coaches ran between Liverpool and Manchester each weekday, carrying more than 600 passengers at up to 12 miles per hour. The journey could be done in less than three hours, one-tenth of the shortest of the circuitous canal routes, but the competition for business between coaching companies led to unwise speeds and many accidents.

By 1821, Joseph Sandars eagerly greeted any investment that might forge a more efficient passage between Lancashire and the docks. He acted from personal interest and a wider concern: well regarded locally for his civic pride and reformist Whig politics, he supported almost all plans for social and economic advance. The link between the textile mills of Manchester and the docks at Liverpool would only be the most visible and direct beneficiary: the prodigious output of the Yorkshire clothiers, the Cheshire salt refineries and the Staffordshire potteries would all use the route into Liverpool, and the steamship route from Ireland greatly improved the livestock trade into Britain. Importers of spice, oil, coffee, tobacco, turpentine, saltpetre, brimstone and dyewood would also all swiftly flourish on an iron rail; Sandars' corn trade would prosper along with the rest.

In his younger days, Sandars had read how several schemes to build an extended rail link between his home town and Manchester had foundered on lack of interest and disbelief. As early as 1797 a canal builder called William Jessop had talked of horses pulling wagons on an iron track along the Lancashire – Cheshire border, but his vision drew little support and no finance. A year later, the engineer Benjamin Outram did manage to interest a group of Manchester businessmen in a more northerly route, but this went nowhere beyond the initial survey. The most successful attempt came in 1820 from Thomas Gray, who wrote a clear-sighted pamphlet and many letters to the newspapers envisaging the whole country joined by rails, with the Liverpool – Manchester route just the most straightforward starting place. Gray believed that no merchant or banker in the neighbouring counties could fail to see the expediency of such an undertaking, but his plans failed for want of a resilient backer, and for the lack of the meeting of minds that occurred just one year later.

It was in 1821 that Sandars met a man named William James, and the two set about transforming the country. James had trained as a solicitor, and often referred to himself as a miner and engineer, but he had made his fortune as a land speculator, draining marshes, supervising property development for earls and lords, and planning new routes for roads and small goods railways. James saw no reason why a more ambitious line should not be constructed between Liverpool and Manchester; he had many such schemes, most of which failed to materialise, but in Joseph Sandars he met an ambitious and influential conspirator who had little experience of project management, and less of engineering works, and thus was ideally placed to underestimate the vast political, financial and technical turmoils that lay ahead.

In 1822, Sandars paid James £300 to conduct a detailed survey between the two towns, and the route that emerged was curvy and hilly. It was not within James's brief or ability to consider how horse-drawn wagons would negotiate steep inclines, much less how steam engines might manage them; most likely a pulley system could be arranged. James had other problems to consider, chief among which was how not to be murdered. His surveying team would frequently be attacked with stones and lumps of coal, and some miners from St Helens formed a lynch mob. The man bearing the theodolite invariably came off worst, and James saw fit to hire protection in the form of a local prizefighter (whose very presence incited protesters to double their efforts). Eventually James and his men conducted their work by moonlight, when they believed they would be less subject to assault. But as their route itself didn't deviate, the Duke of Bridgewater's servants attempted to disrupt even these midnight sojourns by firing shots into the air. It was not always clear what the objectors feared from the survey, beyond the unknown. James found it fruitless to explain that the value of their land might increase, and that the market for their coals would double.

The canal owners were another matter. 'I have been the object of their persecution of hate,' James observed in a letter to Sandars:

They would immolate me if they could; but if I can die the death of Samson, by pulling away the pillars, I am content to die with these Philistines. Be assured, my dear sir, that not a moment shall be lost, nor shall my attention for a day be diverted from this concern, which increases in importance every hour, as well as in the certainty of ultimate success.

James's mission, if not his boundless optimism, was soon disclosed in the local newspapers. In all the reports, civic pride was prominent. In July 1822, the *Manchester Guardian* reflected James's own writings by stating that the proposed iron rail would run from Manchester to Liverpool, while a week later the *Liverpool Mercury* reversed the direction. Both reports suggested that there would soon be public meetings to discuss the proposals, and that an early application would be brought before Parliament.

In truth, James's survey was taking much longer than he liked to admit, and it would be well over a year before an application was made. The newspapers failed to mention two details that would later become significant. One of James's young surveyors under bombardment from missiles was Robert Stephenson; and his newest partner in a business scheme promoting what some still liked to call the Loco Motive was Robert's father George.

FANNY KEMBLE'S journey on the railway, a few days before it opened, was designed as a trial run for its engineers (a last check on mechanics and maintenance), but it was also a chance for coquetry. She travelled up front on a beautiful day at the end of August, still but for the breeze in her ribboned hair as the engine picked up steam. Her guide was a noteworthy man, 'rather stern-featured . . . with a dark and deeply marked countenance' and a certain apprehension that his entire world would collapse if his staggering venture fell short of expectations.

George Stephenson had met Charles Kemble, a friend of several of the railway's directors, and had asked his family and friends aboard on 25 August 1830 for a 15-mile glide halfway to Manchester. On this day, the railway no longer belonged to Sandars and James, but to George Stephenson alone. Stephenson spoke in a fat Northumbrian brogue that struck some listeners as Scottish, preferring 'noo' to 'now' (once, it was said, he was asked what would happen if his steam locomotive met a cow, and he figured it would be an unfortunate meeting 'for the coo'). His tale of perseverance struck twenty-one-year-old Fanny Kemble as a 'wonderful history, as much more interesting than a romance as truth is stranger than fiction.' When this truth was related by Stephenson himself, 'while his tame dragon flew panting along his iron pathway with us,' she found it comparable in fantasy to the *Arabian Nights*.

Before being escorted up to the boilerplate, Kemble was ushered into a large courtyard 'where, under cover, stood several carriages of a peculiar construction,' one of which was made ready for her journey.

Fanny Kemble, the fearless phenomenon.

It was a long-bodied vehicle with seats placed across it, back to back; the one we were in had six of these benches . . . The wheels were placed upon two iron bands, which formed the road, and to which they are fitted, being so constructed as to slide along without any danger of hitching or becoming displaced, on the same principle as a thing sliding on a concave groove.

The carriage was set in motion by a mere push, and, having received this impetus, rolled with us down an inclined plane into a tunnel, which forms the entrance to the railroad. This tunnel is four hundred yards long (I believe) and will be lighted by gas. At the end of it we emerged from darkness.

At the end of the tunnel, Kemble was introduced to the engine which was to drag her along the rails,

the whole machine not bigger than a common fire engine. She goes upon two wheels, which are her feet, and are moved by bright steel legs called pistons; these are propelled by steam, and in proportion as more steam is applied to the common extremities (the hip-joints, I suppose) of these pistons, the faster they move the wheels.

The horse analogy was Stephenson's own, and it predicted an anthropomorphic outbreak that exists to the present day; if a machine moves, we have difficulty in seeing it as just a machine. 'His way of explaining himself is peculiar,' Kemble reasoned, 'but very striking, and I understood, without difficulty, all that he said to me.' She thought Stephenson slightly older than his years, at between fifty and fifty-five (he was forty-nine). His face was careworn and thoughtful; his language had not the slightest touch of vulgarity or coarseness. Kemble told her friend Harriet St Leger that she was 'most horribly in love'.

Back at the track,

the reins, bit and bridle of this wonderful beast is a small steel handle, which applies or withdraws the steam from its legs or pistons, so that a child might manage it. The coals, which are its oats, were under the bench, and there was a small glass tube affixed to the boiler, with water in it, which indicates by its fullness or emptiness when the creature wants water, which is immediately conveyed to it from its reservoirs. There is a chimney to the stove, but as they burn coke there is none of the dreadful black smoke which accompanies the progress of a steam-vessel. This snorting little animal, which I felt rather inclined to pat, was then harnessed to our carriage, and, Mr Stephenson having taken me on the bench of the engine with him, we started at about ten miles an hour . . .

WITH WILLIAM JAMES out planning his railway, Sandars sought influential support in Liverpool and Manchester, establishing a provisional committee that would include bankers, tradesmen, speculators, landowners and solicitors, each of them a politician in their own field, most with a little to gain beyond the plain heady allure of hitching themselves to any new mechanical project in this confident age. Sandars first approached his friends, and they approached theirs; most didn't need much persuading as to the necessity of a railroad, although few were prepared to risk their own fortune on such an extravagant venture. The first committee contained about twice as many representatives from Liverpool than Manchester, and so it remained for the duration of the project. From the start it was clear that the home of the railway was by the water. The headquarters of the operation and the most dramatic new structural edifices would all be in Liverpool. As Sandars gathered his men for their first large meeting at the offices of the Liverpool solicitors Pritt and Clay in 1822, none yet dared visualise a festive banquet on opening day, but none would have doubted its location.

Among the most vocal and clear-sighted in that first meeting was John Moss, a Justice of the Peace with his own thriving independent bank, just the kind of powerful local figure Sandars was looking for. He was joined by John Gladstone, an MP who ran a fleet of trading ships between Liverpool and his coffee and sugar plantations in the West Indies. Gladstone was good friends with William Huskisson, being instrumental in his selection as a parliamentary candidate for Liverpool in 1823.

Henry Booth, who hoped for the best.

Two other friends of Huskisson, both wealthy local merchants, joined the committee at the start: Sir John Tobin and William Ewart. When the provisional committee became an official company in 1824, they were joined by its administrator Henry Booth and by the Liverpool Mayor Charles Lawrence, another friend of Huskisson's who was swiftly elected as the company's first chairman.

Together they signed the first prospectus. This was an eloquent and beguiling document composed predominantly by Henry Booth in the first weeks of October 1824. Its claims were upon 'public encouragement' and it proposed a railway for the same reason that other men had once proposed canals: as the best mode of transport for the times.

Booth and Lawrence anticipated fierce opposition not just from canal owners, but from those whose land would be ploughed up in the name of progress. They would not be disappointed. The Railway Company claimed it had selected its route with speed in mind but also with regard to causing the least inconvenience to the local land interests. A crudely drawn plan was attached to the prospectus, from which, Booth and Lawrence hoped, it would

be perceived that the [rail] road does not approach within about a mile and a half of the residence of the Earl of Sefton, and that it traverses the Earl of Derby's property over the barren mosses of Kirby and Knowsley, passing about two miles distance from the hall.

There followed a comparison between the costs and speed of canal and rail between the two towns, with the conservative rail estimate of four to five hours reflecting the directors' view that the ideal line would combine locomotive engines, fixed engines pulling carriages by ropes, and horses. There would be several further benefits of a railway. The canals suffered from the uncertainties of weather: a shortage of water in the summer obliged barges to carry half loads, while the frosts of winter could lock up traffic for a month. Goods that would take twenty-one days to arrive in Liverpool from New York and Boston could then take as long again to make the additional few miles to Lancashire. Then there was the pilferage, the common thefts afforded so many opportunities during the long and dilatory passage (before goods could travel from Liverpool on the canals to Manchester, they first had to travel up the Mersey to

Runcorn, a journey of almost twenty miles, stretching the working distance between the two towns from thirty to fifty miles).

It was proposed that the railway would swiftly benefit from the addition of branch lines. The wealthy town of Bolton would be well served, as would the mining villages surrounding St Helens, at present a thirty-mile detour by water along the Sankey Canal and down the Mersey (a rail link would halve the present thirty-hour journey). The cost of coal would be reduced; and the cost of other traffic on the railway would be reduced by the additional income from coals. It was suggested that the railroad would greatly improve the prosperity of Ireland, as demand for all her agricultural products would multiply in the large mainland markets at Lancaster and York.

The prospectus concluded with a flourish, and a threat. 'Let it not . . . be imagined that were England to be tardy, other countries would pause in the march of improvement.' The Emperor of Russia had already requested a copy of the plans and the design of the engines; in the United States there was much interest in the proposed line, and an individual had recently been seen in Liverpool gathering information for his own rail link between the great rivers Potomac and Ohio (in fact, many Americans had come to town that year, taking note of gauges, boiler designs and speeds). In this way was the national interest called to account, an issue which those members of Parliament whose assent was required for such a prominent undertaking would surely find difficult to shirk. The railway 'will afford a stimulus to the productive industry of the country,' Henry Booth wrote. It would

give a new impulse to the powers of accumulation, the value and importance of which can be fully understood only by those who are aware how seriously commerce may be impeded by petty restrictions, and how commercial enterprise is encouraged and promoted by an adherence to principles of fair competition, and free trade.

The prospectus ran to over 2,000 words. Only thirty-two of these, towards the end, considered the potential for passenger travel. The Railway held out 'the fair prospect of a public accommodation,' its principal directors believed, but its 'magnitude and importance . . . cannot be immediately ascertained.'

T HE HUSKISSONS TRAVELLED by horse-drawn coach from Cowes to their residence in the village of Eartham, near Chichester, at the end of August, staying for a week before setting off for Liverpool. His friends noticed that the sea air had worked its charms, and that the MP looked better than they could ever remember, though he still felt wretched. On 1 September, he had tried a spot of pheasant shooting (his favourite pastime), but even lifting his gun had tired him, and he returned within an hour with a nervous complaint and the belief that his strength had been sapped from him for good. He was daunted by his forthcoming list of engagements.

William Wainewright, his private secretary, had received so many requests for Huskisson's attendance at banquets and ceremonies that the few he had accepted on his behalf seemed the meanest of concessions. But when Huskisson arrived in Liverpool, Wainewright feared that even one may prove an imposition.

The journey lasted more than a week, a trail of horse-coaches that took the couple from Eartham on the 4th, stopping for the night at his friends Sturges Bourne and Edward Littleton, arriving at Lord Stafford's at Trentham on the 8th. For two days Huskisson was confined to bed, but then travelled on to Sir John Tobin's at Oak Hill, Liverpool, where a party of friends greeted him with delight and relief.

Emily Huskisson had never been to this town before and her husband was eager to show what it had become in recent years.

On Monday 13 September the couple took a pleasure trip on the Mersey, whereupon Mrs Huskisson noted in her journal how

we embarked early in one of the steamboats . . . in order that I might have the opportunity of seeing to the best advantage those magnificent docks and quays of Liverpool, those wonderful emporiums of her wealth and industry.

She was informed that the dock trade would double with the opening of the railway, but she wrote that she found it difficult to imagine how this expansion could be accommodated. In the afternoon, with her husband called away on political business, Emily Huskisson was persuaded to visit the magnificent public cemetery, where she was promised a landmark in memorial splendour. Huskisson personally urged her to visit this spot, and she went though fatigued, and expressed herself impressed with her visit though puzzled by its purpose. The cemetery, consecrated eighteen months before, stood in the shadow of St James's church at one end of Hope Street, and was known locally for its catacombs and the Doric architecture of its small chapel. A few days later, it would be known throughout the country as something else, the place where Mrs Huskisson agreed to bury her husband.

The day after her visit to the new public cemetery, Mrs Huskisson recovered at home. Her husband, who said he was feeling fine again, journeyed out with Sir John Tobin, John Bolton and other friends and walked upon the trading exchange. Here men bartered shares and dealt in cotton, sugar, rum, rice, pigs, tar and indigo, and on this particular day some tried to obtain tickets for the opening of the railway. And then among them came their infirm returning idol, a champion of local interests, the very truest definition of the modern statesman. His tumultuous reception spoke plainly of his constituents' adulation. Many greeted him with comments about how well he was looking.

A man from the *Liverpool Courier* was plainly deceived by Huskisson's ability to summon inner strength while on public display. 'It gives us great pleasure to state that the health of our highly esteemed representative is so far restored that he has not only been enabled to perform the journey from his residence to Liverpool . . . but that he has given them the most unequivocal evidence of the benefit which he has received from his sojourn in the Isle of Wight.'

By the time of his visit at 3.30 p.m., the large Exchange Room was so crowded that no one present could recall a larger gathering. Huskisson was never more welcome, the journalist reported, 'and we are persuaded that there never was a period when his observations were listened to with a deeper interest.'

When the cheers died, Huskisson spoke of his regret at missing the election, 'almost the first, I believe, in modern times in which a member for Liverpool has been restored to the confidence of his constituents without making his appearance among them at the hustings.' During his illness he had sent the freemen a letter containing what he fondly called his General Principles required to improve the country's wellbeing. These concerned lessening 'the pressure upon the springs of our productive industry', the one axiom that had governed all of Huskisson's recent political work. He campaigned for a reduction in taxation, for an eradication of all monopolies affecting commerce and industry ('the boon which [a monopoly] affords to the privileged party is very far from being the measure of the injury which it inflicts upon all the rest of the community'), and to provide the greatest support possible to the expansion and development of all improvements brought about by the progress of knowledge and the discoveries of science.

'Gentlemen,' his address resumed,

this loyal town is about to receive the visit of a distinguished individual of the highest station and influence in the affairs of this great country. I rejoice that he is coming among you. I am sure that what he has already seen in

27

this county, and what he will see here, will not fail to make a great impression on his mind. After this visit he will be better enabled to estimate the value and importance of Liverpool in the general scale of the great interests of this country. He will see what can be effected by patient and persevering industry, by enterprise, and good sense ...

They were to be visited by the Duke of Wellington, the Prime Minister, who at that precise moment was on a coach bound for Liverpool so that he may open the railway. He would find a city with much poverty but much improvement, a merchant community flourishing by virtue of free trade and a lack of restrictive monopoly.

He will see that you know how to thrive and prosper without it; that all you expect from Government is encouragement, protection, facility, and freedom in your several pursuits and avocations, either of manufacturing industry or commerce ...

'I rejoice at the change for the better,' Huskisson concluded, referring to the recent upturn in the economy and the fortunes of business.

I hope and believe it will be permanent. In foreign countries you have powerful rivals to encounter; and you can only hope to continue your superiority over them by incessantly labouring to lighten the pressure upon the industry of our own people, and by promoting every measure which is calculated to give increased vigour, fresh life, and greater facility to the powers which create, and to the hands which distribute, the almost boundless productions of this great country.

And this was really only the beginning, he believed, for the railway would usher in a further period of prosperity, and within short years a mesh of trading channels that would bring the goods presently unloading at the Mersey docks to every market in the world with as much eagerness as hot blood coursing through the human body.

More applause at the end of his speech, followed by a short visit to the Underwriters' Room. When he left the building he shook so many hands that his own became sore. Further cheers greeted his arrival at the King's Arms, where he had the rare opportunity of viewing the town's second most popular local attraction, the nineteen-year-old Siamese twins Chang and Eng, installed in the ballroom.

T HE SKY WAS BRIGHTENING. For John Moss and the other directors assembled at the company offices in Crown Street it was already a day of triumph, whatever the ensuing hours might bring. They had received word that the Duke had arrived in Liverpool safely, and was on his way, though there appeared to be some delay. As they waited, they were encouraged by the huge crowds and the morning's papers.

Liverpool enjoyed a prosperous newspaper trade, and in one week a resident might decide between the *Courier*, the *Mercury*, the *Journal*, the *Albion* and the *Liverpool Times*, and while there was little to divide them on subject matter, they each twisted a Whiggish or Tory knife. Advertisements and proclamations anchored the front pages. Mr Gray, of the Royal College of Surgeons, announced his annual trip from London to Liverpool to fit clients with false teeth, which were fixed 'by capillary attraction and the pressure of the atmosphere, thereby avoiding pinning to stumps, tieing, twisting wires . . .' Courses improving handwriting were popular, as were new treatments for bile, nervous debility and slow fevers. The Siamese twins at the King's Arms Hotel were proving such a draw that they were remaining in Liverpool until Saturday 25th, when, according to their promoter Captain Coffin, 'they must positively leave'. The day's papers carried news of a special medal to commemorate the opening of the railway, 'a beautiful and highly-finished production that leaves its competitors far behind'. A copy in gold had already been sent to the Duke of Wellington, Sir Robert Peel and Mr Huskisson.

Crime and misadventure featured prominently. Accidents were invariably 'melancholy'. In the week of the railway opening, the papers had news of a melancholy event in central London, of a young man named James Rogers, a porter employed by Mr Benson, a grocer in Tottenham Court Road.

The unfortunate young man was crossing Oxford-street, carrying a heavy load, when he was suddenly knocked down by a large carriage dog that ran with great force between his legs, and most unfortunately at the same instant a cart was passing loaded with bricks, the wheel of which passed over his leg and thigh, which were fractured in a most shocking manner before the carman had any power of stopping his horse.

There was so much sudden blood that another dog stopped to drink it. Assistance was immediately rendered to Rogers, and he was conveyed in a most deplorable condition to the hospital, where his family met him with long faces.

Some of the papers reflected the weary early struggle of the railway and its attendant parliamentary warfare, thus lending an even grander air of triumph to today's opening. Railway stewards called on soldiers from the 4th Regiment to hold back the crowds; it appeared that the entire town of Liverpool was converging on Crown Street, and that everyone from the countryside had spread themselves along the route. The air was greasy and sweet, the ground still damp from the night's rain; the forecast was fair, with more rain expected by the evening, but by then it was believed everyone would be safely home.

'Never was there such an assemblage of rank, wealth, beauty, and fashion in this neighbourhood,' one local reporter observed. And there was triumphal music at every turn,

the band of the 4th King's Own Regiment . . . playing military airs, the Wellington Harmonic Band, in a Grecian car for the procession, performing many beautiful miscellaneous pieces, and a third band occupying a stage above Mr Harding's grandstand, at William the Fourth's Hotel, spiritedly adding to the liveliness of the hour whenever the other bands ceased.

But the Duke of Wellington had still not appeared as expected by 9.30, and it was said he had indulged himself the night before. In fact he had spent a quiet evening with friends in Childwall, recovering from his recent excursions in Manchester. It had already been quite a week for the Duke, and it was only Wednesday. The previous Saturday he had been met at the Manchester coach office by an open carriage drawn by four horses – a carriage sent by his host for a few days, the Earl of Wilton – and the Duke paraded alone through the town on his way to the Earl's residence, Heaton Park. It hadn't been a smooth ride. Although most onlookers cheered him on this solitary journey, he also received hisses and boos, and they had grown from one individual on the steps of the Albion Hotel to a noisy chorus by the time he reached Stockport.

On Sunday he attended Prestwich Church, where the minister preached an apt sermon from St Luke's gospel: 'Woe unto you if all men speak well of you, for so did their fathers to the false prophets.' On Monday he toured factories and attended a gala banquet at the Theatre Royal, an awkward evening in which 750 men ate and proposed toasts from tables set up in a tent in the audience section and from a marquee on the stage. The Duke of Wellington noted that the president for the night was Manchester's chief magistrate, who talked of the importance of maintaining a steady police force to uphold the progress of commerce. Wellington, of course, had an eye on revolution in Paris and the abdication of Charles X. Succeeding him, the Earl of Wilton spoke of how public opinion was moving with rapid strides 'in a course which, if unchecked, would be attended with considerable danger.' People just weren't as obedient or respectful as once they were.

31

Several factors had placed the Duke of Wellington's government in a precarious state. The Duke himself faced pressures from within – not least from Huskisson's liberal Tory faction demanding a more tolerant, reforming outlook. And the mood of unease he had just witnessed in the streets, a revolutionary spirit inspired by the uprisings in France and Belgium, had no more certain local manifestation than the Manchester cotton workers who had taken to wearing exotic cockades decorated with the shades of the *tricoleur*. The Manchester 'Peterloo' massacre of 1819 – in which eleven people were killed and hundreds injured when the cavalry was used to disperse a vast but peaceful crowd demanding widespread reforms – was still fresh in the memory, and the clamour for parliamentary representation and a widening of the franchise was intense. Remarkably, Manchester returned no MPs to Parliament, while a tiny area like Newton, a mid-point on the Liverpool and Manchester line, returned two. The Duke was keeping a lid on things, but steam was rattling the rims.

On 9 September, Lord Charles Greville, clerk of the Privy Council for forty years and horse trader to King George IV, captured the mood in his diary. 'Nothing can exceed the interest, the excitement, the consternation which prevail here,' he wrote after visiting Lancashire. 'As we went down on Saturday, Henry [his brother] told me that there had been alarming accounts from the manufacturing districts of a disposition to rise on the part of the workmen.'

Greville met his brother-in-law Lord Francis Egerton, later to be the Earl of Ellesmere, the proprietor of the Bridgewater Canal.

He takes a gloomy view of everything, not a little perhaps tinctured by the impending ruin which he foresees to his own property from the Liverpool Railroad, which is to be opened with great ceremony on the 15th; moreover he thinks the government so weak that it cannot stand, and expects the Duke will be compelled to resign.

A day later, Greville made another entry. 'I think the alarmists are increasing everywhere, and the signs of the times are certainly portentous.'

And so it was that the opening of the railway had come at the perfect moment for the Duke of Wellington, for he planned to use it to celebrate Britain's standing in the world. Fifteen years after his glories at Waterloo, jingoism still had its uses. There was irony here, for the railway conveyed the one thing Wellington distrusted the most: the rapid dissemination of new ideas.

It was arranged for the public dinners at the opening ceremonies to be packed with Tory supporters, and this had been evident at the Theatre Royal in Manchester a few nights before. But on that evening it was also clear that not all of Wellington's friends were keen on the railway. The Earl of Wilton, who had been one of its chief opponents from its inception, spoke repeatedly of his unshakable vision of doom.

AFTER HIS TRIUMPHS of the previous night, Huskisson awoke with a common malady, a sore head from wine. At 7.30 he arose in an unfamiliar bedroom at Wavertree Hall, the residence of Charles Lawrence, the chairman of the railway.

How did Huskisson feel? Clearly not well, but he had always enjoyed the ability to raise his spirits on demand, and on the day of this grand opening, with himself as much the conquering hero as the Duke, he moved to the washroom for his ablutions.

The mirror showed a man older than his sixty years. That Huskisson had been intermittently unwell since his youth was now more than apparent. It was a frailty he masked with a keen interest in sports and walking, but it laid him low for weeks at a time. In recent years he walked with a stiffened elbow that caused one friend to detect a marked alteration in the spirit and elasticity of his carriage. The frequency of his accidents, coupled with chronic internal episodes of gout, 'had given rise to a certain hesitation in his movements wherever any crowd or obstacle impeded him . . .'

It would require an unduly cynical perspective to suggest that Huskisson's undivided support of the new railway had much to do with his misfortunes with horses and their carriages, but he did profess to be awaiting the day when journeying would be less jolting to the constitution.

The commemorative medal: a train traverses the Sankey Viaduct.

THE DUKE OF WELLINGTON appeared at the Crown Street offices just before ten, accompanied by the Marquis and Marchioness of Salisbury, the Marchioness leaning on his arm. He was all in black, still respectful of the death of the King, but it was an outfit pomped up with a black Spanish cloak. Simultaneously, the three bands struck up 'See The Conquering Hero Comes'. He was widely cheered despite his tardiness; the directors found it hard to suppress their relief, at his arrival and his reception.

Those with tickets had a little adventure assigned to them – the task of finding their particular carriage. There were eight locomotives in all, and with the exception of the Duke of Wellington's engine, *Northumbrian*, were each parading their own coloured silk flag: for the *Phoenix* it was dark green, the *North Star*'s was yellow, the *Rocket* light blue, the *Dart* purple, the *Comet* deep red, the *Arrow* pink and the *Meteor* brown. Their names suggested fleetness and celestial guidance, while the *Northumbrian* was named after its engineer's birthplace. The flag colours enabled spectators to identify them as they passed, and helped the 700 passengers locate their seats: their tickets displayed a corresponding colour. Once settled, the coaches released their brakes and ran by gravity through a 300-yard tunnel, at the end of which they entered a terminus and were attached to their engines. The engines themselves had no brakes, and could be stopped only by the driver reversing the valve-gear, a process that took several seconds to effect and many more to complete.

On this one day, the trains would be travelling to Manchester on both sets of tracks, side by side. The *Northumbrian* would pull the Duke of Wellington and his guests on one track, while the other seven locomotives would proceed in one line on the parallel. There was a logic to this arrangement: the Prime Minister and his friends could steam up and down as they pleased, inspecting the railway's landmarks as their interest allowed, while they in turn were

35

inspected by the populace. The Duke's grand carriages were full before the rest and so they trundled back and forth to view the other trains on the other track, which gave, as one newspaper reported, 'the assembled thousands and tens of thousands the opportunity of seeing distinctly the illustrious strangers, whose presence gave extraordinary interest to the scene'. Most had never seen the Prime Minister before, nor the princes and envoys and MPs who sat excitedly behind him.

The parade suited his engine driver too, George Stephenson, who soaked up the cheers and gasps with the occasional wave of his hat. One passenger assigned a seat in a carriage drawn by the *Phoenix* was delighted to find his engine leading the procession on the other line. The *Phoenix* consisted of three open and two covered carriages, each carrying twenty-six passengers. 'A few minutes before eleven all was ready for the journey,' he remembered, 'and certainly a journey upon a railway is one of the most delightful that can be imagined.'

Another traveller, a correspondent for the *Mechanics' Magazine*, seemed disgruntled when he found himself in the *Arrow*, last but one in the procession. He noted the constables and soldiers 'keeping the railway clear, and impressing on the multitude some regard for their lives and limbs.' He perused the track and the engines, and noted that they were all made by Robert Stephenson and Co. He wondered about the absence of two other engines from London, made by men called Braithwaite and Ericsson, concluding that they had not yet been tested, and the directors no doubt deciding, 'it would not be prudent to allow them to make part of a procession which it was of the utmost consequence should be exposed to as few risks of failure as possible.'

The reporter remarked on the almost boundless power about to be put into operation.

H ENRY BOOTH had been at the railway offices for about an hour by the time the others arrived, his gun upsetting the even hang of his long jacket. He seemed to know everyone. He greeted Charles and Harriet Arbuthnot, Joseph Sandars, Charles Blacker Vignoles, the Stephensons, Charles Lawrence, Viscount Melbourne, Sir Robert Peel, Charles Babbage, Viscount Grey, the Russian Ambassador Count Potocki, the Austrian Ambassador Prince Esterhazy, the United States Consul Francis B Ogden, Edward John Littleton MP, General Gascoyne MP, Sir George Drinkwater (the Mayor of Liverpool), Lord Monson, Lord Clive, Lord Grosvenor, Lord Talbot, Lord Harrowby, the Earl of Brecknock, the Earl of Winton, the Earl and Countess of Wilton, the High Bailiff of Birmingham, the Vicar of Eccles, Dr Brandreth, Dr Southey, William and Emily Huskisson, and finally the Duke of Wellington and cortege. Liverpool had never hosted the aristocracy in such numbers; they had been promised a day of significance.

Booth left the office for a while to walk through the short tunnel towards the locomotives. The drivers were dressed in fine waistcoats and new shoes for the occasion, but spits of flame were already boring holes in the glossy leather. Booth shook their hands on their hissing footplates. There was some nervousness with the excitement, a desire to meet expectations. In the general clatter, for reasons unknown, could be heard an occasional bang.

Booth gave a little speech to a group of newspaper reporters, the same conquering message he had carried for years. Speed, dispatch, distance are still relative terms, but their meaning has been totally changed within a few months, he said. 'What was quick is now slow; what was distant is now near; and this change in our ideas will not be limited to the environs of Liverpool and Manchester.'

The crowd were proud to be a part of history themselves, happy to admire Booth's scaffold of rhetoric. 'There can be no question that foreign countries will adopt the railway communication as one great step in mechanical improvement and commercial enterprise,' Booth informed them.

The country of the Pyramids, of Memphis, and of Thebes, shall then be celebrated for railways and steam carriages; the land of the proud Mameluke or the wandering Arab, of sphinxes and mummies, will become the theatre of mechanical invention, science and the arts. The stately Turk, with his turban and slippers, will quit his couch and his carpet to mount his engine of fire and speed, that he may enjoy the delight of modern locomotion. From west to east, and from north to south, the mechanical principle, the philosophy of the nineteenth century, will spread and extend itself. The world has received a new impulse.

The full carriages descended through the Liverpool tunnel to be affixed to their engines. And then, at twenty minutes to eleven, Henry Booth passed his heavy gun to a local dignitary, who treated it just like a starting pistol and fired one fearsome shot towards heaven. But the official starting signal came the next moment from a nearby cannon, its ecstatic blast flying over and beyond the rails towards a bystander, its cladding hitting him in the face and dislodging an eyeball so that it hung by its moist sinews on his cheek. So this was the beginning – a hat-hoisting hurrah and the day's first misadventure. The acclaim of the crowd rose like a wild wave on the Irish Sea. The fired-up locomotives began to roll towards Manchester.

PART TWO

Without Sinking

The great work of the Liverpool and Manchester Rail-way, advancing towards completion, seemed, by a common unanimity of opinion, to be deemed as the experiment which was to decide the fate of railways. The eyes of the whole scientific world were upon that great undertaking.

Nicholas Wood, Killingworth colliery manager, Robert Stephenson's
first employer, 1832

CHANGING THE COURSE of history is seldom something one can do in a single debate, but there were days at Westminster when the railwaymen attempted to cast the future of a nation.

In October 1824, members of both Houses of Parliament received a letter with a cumbersome title but a direct message. 'On the Subject of the Projected Rail Road between Liverpool and Manchester, Pointing out the Necessity for its Adoption and the Manifest Advantages it Offers to the Public' had been composed by Joseph Sandars in a convincing, confident and angry style. Sandars was no engineer, but he was a slick provincial politician and a stylish propagandist.

His letter was mostly concerned with the monopolistic practices of the canal owners and their exorbitant charges, but then he switched to a positive tack. 'The Rail-road possesses decidedly intrinsic advantages over a Canal conveyance,' Sandars wrote,

a few of which I will endeavour to point out. It is computed that goods could be carried for considerably less than is NOW charged, and for half of what HAS been charged; and that they would be conveyed in one sixth of the time . . .

The canal owners had recently dropped their prices in anticipation of this battle, but they could not increase their speed.

Sandars then ran through the arguments already familiar from Booth's prospectus: cheaper (half-price!); faster (10 – 12 miles per hour, up to 4 miles per hour quicker than horse-drawn coaches!); independent of extreme weather (railways would run unhindered by any natural obstacle and certainly not drought!). He referred his readers to the losses occurred in the great storms of November 1821 and December 1822, when more than fifty vessels were lost or stranded.

'Of its success no doubt can be entertained,' he wrote, although doubts were entertained every hour.

In short, it appears to me that the application for a Rail-Road would be irresistible. That the two [canal] Companies will endeavour to rouse every sort of opposition there can be no question: they will endeavour to alarm the whole body of Canal Proprietors of the kingdom ... As to the Landed Proprietors, there is not an individual who will not be immensely benefited by the Railway passing upon or within a mile or two of his grounds ... the railway will enable him to fertilise his land with the limestone of Wales and Derbyshire, at a considerable reduction on the present cost; it will enable him to get manure from the large towns at a cheaper rate ...

His letter contained details of a petition signed by 150 Liverpool merchants and brokers declaring their difficulties in obtaining suitable vessels to convey their goods to Manchester: they considered the existing transport injurious to the trade of the country. Wary that they should be seen to be acting beyond their immediate trading interests, Sandars added that less than a third of the signatories were also shareholders in his railroad company. But the shareholders had their own part to play, attaching their own 'memorials' to Sandars' plea.

Your memorialists further beg to urge, that by the Rail-road system delays from floods, droughts, frosts or storms can never occur; that goods will escape damage by water, and that the owners will be exposed to no risk by wreck, or from any other cause.

A little further, Sandars again acknowledged the battle to come.

It is not likely that such a measure as the establishment of a Rail-road will pass without contention. Every improvement has been opposed by some one, and yet improvements have gone on. The inhabitants in the vicinity

The mechanic Charles Sylvester, Joseph Sanders and George Stephenson,
who got their way in the end.

of London at one time petitioned Parliament to prevent the extension of
turnpike-roads: – they wanted to continue in possession of the monopoly
of supplying that city with their own produce.

Sandars' letter reached its conclusion with a full and eloquent
blast. 'What has been the effect of Canals?' he asked.

They have increased trade, commerce and manufactures – they have increased turnpike roads – they have increased the number of horses, and the growth of hay and corn – they have increased both the coasting trade and the number of seamen. Canals have done well for the country, just as high roads and pack horses had done before Canals were established; but the country has now presented to it, in this instance, a cheaper and more expeditious mode of conveyance, and the attempt to prevent its adoption is utterly hopeless.

Are the powers of the human mind to be controlled – are its efforts to be restrained by a small body of men, for the protection of their own comparatively insignificant interest? Are their pools of water to form the boundary beyond which science and art shall not be applied . . .?

Sandars noted that there was already railway competition from abroad. If the railroad should be stopped, the country would fall behind in all forms of production and trade.

The Emperor of Russia has obtained a model of the Loco-motive Engine, and at the present moment he has a professional agent investigating the Rail-roads of the north. The Americans, too, are alive to the subject, and at the seat of government it is undergoing discussion. Letters just received from Washington are full of inquiries upon it.

Sandars had followed the improvements of the steam engine with awe and alacrity, concerned that the speed of progress would leave all but the most quick-witted in its wake. Every year there were major innovations and key refinements, and the application of steam had already reconfigured the working landscape. Factories sprung up wherever production demanded, no longer tied to the location of water. New housing went up in great haste by the new factories, but it was Sandars' hope that the steam train would make such proximity unnecessary. He believed that the railways might disfigure the country far less than the other applications of steam had already done.

Long before the development of the passenger-bearing locomotive, Sandars had seen how the application of fixed steam engines in mines and cotton mills had fired Britain's commercial prosperity. He had certainly read the histories, and would deliver impromptu lectures on how Cornishmen and Frenchmen had collectively forged the new steam-driven world. 'The steam engine has raised the productive powers of this country to an extent which even to ourselves appears wonderful,' he wrote, 'but which our ancestors would have regarded as the idle dream of some visionary.' It enabled Britain to carry on the Napoleonic Wars, and it would be the chief means of paying off its debts. Now there was far-fetched talk of coaches on his Liverpool and Manchester Railway being propelled or dragged along its entire length by travelling engines, and an optimistic belief that passengers would soon regard such a thing as normality. It was years away, but the message was unequivocal: 'How monstrous is the idea that the Canal Proprietors should be protected from the consequences of such a discovery.'

Sandars' lectures went back to Thomas Newcomen, though he could justifiably have gone back to the first steam turbine described by Hero of Alexandria, or the lid rattling on a boiling pot that led to Edward Somerset's Water Commanding Engine in 1663 (a steam-operated pump that claimed to raise water 40 feet). He could have mentioned the Digester pressure-cooker and first steam safety-valve described by Dr Denis Papin in the 1670s, championed by Robert Boyle at a dinner of the fledgling Royal Society in London, a precursor to Papin's vacuum-propelled piston steam engine and the first paddle-steamer. And he probably knew about the work of Thomas Savery, the Devon engineer whose steam water-pump of 1702 featured a new condenser and stopcocks and valves, and would have drained all the copper, tin and iron mines in the country had it been made of stronger materials and the mines not been so deep.

But Joseph Sandars began with Thomas Newcomen's Atmospheric Engine because it had been the principal source of inspiration for James Watt. Like Savery, Newcomen also grew up among the mines of Devon, and had improved Savery's draining pump by increasing the mechanical force obtained from a piston in a cylinder; this improved the condensation of steam with the addition of cold water directly into the base of the steam cylinder, ensuring a faster creation of vacuum and an effective atmospheric downward pressure on the piston.

James Watt's improvements included a lagging of Newcomen's pipes and boiler to improve efficiency, changing much of the machinery from brass to iron, and the addition of a separate condenser to the boiler and cylinder, thus ensuring a more responsive vacuum and greater power for his pistons. His researches with Joseph Black into the latent heat of steam, and his partnership with the Birmingham engineer Matthew Boulton produced the double-acting steam engine of 1787, a fuel-efficient multi-use machine that would stoke all aspects of the Industrial Revolution. Its up-and-down motion would first pump the mines, but within a few years its rotary motion would run the Lancashire cotton mills. The Spinning Jenny and Mule had previously run on water power, but their speed and productivity were now transformed.

Watt was by nature a conservative man, suspicious of many of the ludicrous locomotive schemes envisioned for his engines, but his friends entertained visions of their own. One of them was Erasmus Darwin, father of the naturalist, who met Watt and others each full moon to discuss science and philosophy. They called themselves the Lunar Society, but detractors called them the Lunatics, and for their evidence they pointed to the wild fancies in Darwin's poem, 'The Botanic Garden'.

> Soon shall thy arm, unconquered Steam, afar
> Drag the slow barge, or drive the rapid car;

> Or on wide waving wings expanded bear
> The flying chariot through the field of air.

The Mule, Samuel Crompton's hybrid machine that combined Richard Arkwright's water frame with James Hargreaves' Spinning Jenny to produce great quantities of fine yarn for weaving, had been manufactured for years by John Kennedy, a friend of Joseph Sandars. Sandars enlisted him as a Manchester-based director of his railroad scheme. For years they had witnessed the development of stationary steam engines in manufacturing, and they had seen the slow, heaving beginnings of the application of steam to locomotion. Little private steam railways with their burning, exploding engines had sprung up all over the north of England and Wales to transfer coal and iron at slow speeds to the waterways. A few show engines ran around circular tracks as fairground exhibits. Engineers talked about the potential of locomotive engines all the time, but in 1824 the prospect of travelling great distances behind one of them was akin to the prospect of spaceflight. But still: Sandars had received letters of inquiry from Washington, and the Emperor of Russia had agents wandering about the coalfields of the north.

SEVERAL YEARS EARLIER, William James had taken a break in his survey of marshland and copse to visit Killingworth Colliery in Northumberland, a flourishing mine that had already experienced the advantages of the railroad. Killingworth employed horses to drag wagons along rails from the shafts to the dispatch areas, but now a man called Stephenson was demonstrating something called Blücher, a travelling steam engine that had taken its name from Wellington's Prussian ally against Napoleon.

Its engineer was a man with no formal education, the son of a pit fireman. George Stephenson learnt to read and write at night school

47

after days tending cattle. In his teens he went to work at his father's mine at Dewley Burn near Newcastle Upon Tyne and then at Black Callerton two miles away: his first jobs were predictably menial – ridding coal of stones, driving horses with wagons – but he soon graduated to maintaining the primitive engines in his roles as 'plugman' and 'brakesman', the latter task controlling the rate at which coal was drawn up from the mine to the surface. As a boy he used to build replica engines from clay, and now he had the chance to dismantle and examine them close at hand. He impressed his colleagues with his great strength and ingenuity, and an enquiring mind that would later produce a new method of clock-cleaning and a miner's safety lamp similar to Humphry Davy's. His son Robert later wrote of his father's early attempts at Black Callerton to invent a new engine break, but this was cast aside after his family moved to yet another workplace.

Stephenson made his name at West Moor colliery, Killingworth, about seven miles north of Newcastle, moving there as brakesman in 1804. His first challenge was helping his father recover from an accident (he lost his sight when a co-worker let in steam on an engine he was repairing), and paying off an obligation to join the militia. He considered emigration to the United States, but could not afford the passage. 'You know the road from my house at the West Moor to Killingworth,' he later told a friend. 'I remember once when I went along that road I wept bitterly, for I knew not where my lot in life would be cast.' But matters improved several years later when he discovered his talent for repairing inefficient pit engines. He adjusted pulleys on winding engines and achieved local notoriety when he alone amongst his much older colleagues fixed the fault on a Newcomen pumping engine that was failing to drain the mine. By the time William James visited Killingworth in 1815, Stephenson had become the colliery's engine-wright, and each month was making small but significant adjustments to a locomotive he had built after witnessing great improvements in machines at other local mines. James was impressed with the engine's leverage and speed (up to 8 miles an hour), and he had soon drawn up a business agreement with George Stephenson and his partner William Losh that might profit them all: in return for a quarter share in sales of their next locomotives, James agreed to promote them on the lines he surveyed. In this way, they hoped, steam locomotion would overpower its sceptics to become the symbol of the modern age. Or at the very least it would make them wealthy.

But James appeared to be over-extending himself. In the same period as he was surveying the Liverpool and Manchester line, he had interests in at least five other possible routes, including the Bolton and Leigh Railway, the Portsmouth and Chatham Railway and the Croydon, Merstham and Godstone line, and these in addition to his own schemes to develop a new type of tubular iron rail. His ambition was not matched by his financial management, and in the autumn of 1822 he was thrown in jail for bad debts. He served three months but was back in the King's Bench Prison within the year, from where he tried to reassure Joseph Sandars that all was well, and that he would soon have his survey before Parliament.

But the railway committee was growing impatient, and resolved to take a more active role. In May 1824 Sandars, Henry Booth and two others took a coach north and followed William James's path to the Killingworth colliery. They broke their journey to inspect work on the Stockton and Darlington Railway, a 25-mile route linking the abundant coalfields in the western part of Durham with the market town of Darlington and then eastwards again towards the navigable waterway at Stockton-on-Tees. It consisted of a single line of iron rails, and employed a combination of fixed steam engines, horses and locomotives.

To most people not involved in the project, the Stockton and

Darlington line appeared an unromantic venture, its engines fearsome boilers with mysterious names: Hope, Black Diamond and Diligence. During construction it received a small fraction of the attention the newspapers would later afford the Liverpool and Manchester line, and to those who didn't see it for themselves it remained a rumbling far-off oddity, more of a threat than an excitement.

But Sandars and his friends were impressed and inspired. The line was a magnificent achievement, the culmination of fifteen years' work by the Quaker industrialist Edward Pease. Pease was based in Darlington and had long realised that, unlike many of the deep coalfaces near Newcastle, and Tyne and Wear, his local Durham seams just south of Bishop Auckland were far nearer the surface; it had already been shown that a pit could be sunk, and good quality coal dug out for sale within a week. All that was needed for the mines to be profitable was an expanded market, and an easier way of reaching it. Various horse tramways and canals were proposed before local businessmen seriously considered a railway in 1818.

After initial failure in Parliament, royal assent for this novel venture was granted in 1821, and its complex and hilly construction began, described with awe by a contributor to the *Caledonian Mercury*:

From the collieries at Witton Park and Etherly the coal wagons are conveyed by horses to the foot of Etherly Ridge, a distance of a mile. Here the horses are detached, and the wagons drawn up the north side of the ascent by means of a steam engine which is fixed on the top, and draws a rope that reaches from it to the foot of the hill . . . The wagons descend by their own gravity, and the rope which is attached to them, winding round a barrel at the top, serves to regulate and check their rapid descent . . . From thence a new set of horses draws [the wagons] about a mile and a quarter farther to the foot of Brusselton Hill . . .

Another fixed engine and rope system was in place here, but after it things were fairly level, and the wagons could be hauled all the way to Stockton either by a group of horses or by one locomotive engine. It cost about £150,000. It was the most spectacular demonstration so far of an exceptional and daring engineering mind.

Within a few days of Booth's and Sandars' visit, they had appointed the Stockton and Darlington Railway's chief engineer as their own: George Stephenson. William James learnt of his dismissal during yet another period in prison. Shortly afterwards, Stephenson appointed a principal surveyor, and within days they were both out on the line at the Liverpool end, stealthily checking levels.

The chief surveyor was Paul Padley, a man originally engaged by James. He saw little need to diverge much from the original route, not least because he was under severe pressure to draw up a final set of plans for consideration by the House of Commons within weeks. On his release from prison, William James was offered a less significant role within the Railway Company, which he refused. He wrote to his son: '[Padley] knows my plans of which he and Stephenson will now avail themselves. I confess I did not calculate upon such duplicity in either.'

Like their predecessors, Stephenson and Padley were also forced to survey by moonlight, and the opposition did not soften over time. The most notable change to the route was a little curious, and it must have baffled the railway committee. The railway did not proceed in a straight line eastwards towards Manchester but almost due north, towards Bootle, in an attempt to avoid excessive tunnelling. But Stephenson was straight about two things: he professed a loathing of inclines, suggesting that he had found the rope haulage over those Durham hills ugly but unavoidable; he would, wherever possible, cut through or over troublesome gradients in an attempt to render the line faster and smoother. And he would contemplate going as fast as mechanically possible, using steam locomotives for the entire journey. All of these ambitions would soon lead to the most humiliating day of his life.

HOW WOULD PARLIAMENT respond to a new age? With great alarm and dim-wittedness.

The passage of the Liverpool and Manchester Railway Bill through the committee lasted thirty-eight sessions over ten weeks, from mid-March to the end of May 1825, but the political work of the railway directors began long before the Commons and Lords considered Stephenson's survey. Joseph Sandars and John Gladstone spent the last few weeks of 1824 in the company of Sir John Barrow and Robert Spankie in London, receiving advice on protocol and chicanery. Barrow, Second Secretary to the Admiralty and a leading naval administrator, thought he knew what members of parliament wanted to hear. He advised the railway directors not to frighten them with talk of steam locomotives (horses and fixed engines would not only be regarded as safer, but also within the bounds of their experience) but this advice was ignored; and he told them on no account to mention the possibility of conveying passengers. 'You will at once raise a host of enemies in the proprietors of coaches, post-chaises, innkeepers etc,' he predicted. 'And for what? Some thousands of passengers, you say – but a few hundreds I should say – in the year.'

Robert Spankie was a solicitor, and one of several parliamentary agents engaged by Gladstone to guide the Bill. Initially things appeared to go smoothly. There were many petitions in favour of the 101-page proposal, notably from merchants, shipowners and chambers of commerce in Liverpool, Bradford, Bury, Leeds, York and several towns in Ireland. There was a little opposition to the project in the newspapers, notably from John Edward Taylor, editor of the *Manchester Guardian*, who approved of the railway in

George Stephenson, who stumbled into Parliament.

principle, but not the use of high-pressure engines. He quoted various experts who feared their 'unavoidable insecurity'.

More significantly, a petition against the railway was drawn up by a Liverpool man named John Shaw Leigh, who had found several discrepancies between the Bill submitted to Parliament and the one posted for public inspection: Leigh had noticed either extreme sloppiness or something worse – incompetence. The errors involved such fundamental issues as the precise route of the railway, the bridges and depots to be used and the levels to be made. At first, this petition received little attention.

Within Parliament, high-profile speeches on the Bill came from William Peel (Sir Robert Peel's brother, Member for Tamworth, advocating the railway's boost to trade), John Doherty (Member from County Wexford who believed that commerce between Liverpool and Manchester would soon fill to capacity six canals and six railways) and George Philips (who opposed it on the grounds that the projected travel times must be wrong, as no safe steam locomotive could go faster than five miles an hour).

Despite the calm beginnings, the railway directors were soon confounded not only by the cold blast from canal and landowners, but from paid witnesses who impressed with wild but convincing speculation. From the very start of the project, the first survey had thrown up one fearful problem: Chat Moss. This was a barren stretch not long before Manchester, almost five miles in diameter, a boggy expanse of moor that was deemed impassable in winter by foot or any other means. The Moss had assumed such abysmal and mythical proportions in people's imaginations that its 'quick and faithless depths' were said of late to have accounted for a hundred deaths. Its reputation did the railway supporters no favours in Parliament.

A civil engineer named Francis Giles was called to the Commons in early May to answer a straightforward question: could a railway traverse Chat Moss without sinking?

'I say certainly not.'

'Will it be necessary, therefore, in making a Rail-road which is to stand, to take out, along the whole line of the road, the whole of the Moss to the bottom?'

'Undoubtedly.'

'Will that make it necessary to cut down the 33 or 34 feet of which you have been speaking?'

'Yes . . . No carriage can stand on the Moss short of the bottom.'

Giles, who had wide experience of canals but none of rails, estimated that the excavation of the Moss would cost £200,000, rather more than the £6,000 that railway directors had budgeted for a straight crossing. Giles believed the whole railway would cost as much as £1.5 million, or £900,000 more than Stephenson had estimated.

Giles was a prominent sideshow, but the true star of the committee was Edward Hall Alderson, a court judge well versed in the art of cross-examination. It took Alderson a while to warm up: his questioning of John Rastrick, an engineer who spoke eloquently about the speed, safety and other virtues of the locomotive, failed to dent the railway's case. But by the time he got to work on George Stephenson three days later he was ready for someone's flesh, and he systematically tore the engineer apart.

Stephenson's doughy accent didn't help him, and some members complained that they could hardly understand a word; untutored regional dialects were something they rarely encountered. What they did grasp was not impressive. Stephenson appeared quite unprepared for the detail and ferocity of Alderson's questioning, and seemed ashamed that it exposed so many inadequacies in his land survey. Alderson had picked up on the petition of John Shaw Leigh, and began asking about costs and measurements. 'What is the width of the Irwell there?' he asked harmlessly at one point.

'I cannot say exactly at present,' Stephenson said.

'How many arches is your bridge to have?'

'It is not determined upon.'

'How could you make an estimate for it then?'

'I have given a sufficient sum for it . . .'

It was assumed that Stephenson's interest in the Stockton and Darlington line and other projects had led him to delegate too much of the survey to lesser men; perhaps he had failed to check their work. Several of their calculations were plain wrong, and Stephenson covered up their inadequacies and his own with frequent replies of 'I do not recollect' and 'It was a mistake'. Alderson concluded that Stephenson's performance showed

how utterly and totally devoid he is of common sense . . . His is a mind perpetually fluctuating between opposite difficulties. He neither knows whether he is to make bridges over roads or rivers . . . or embankments, or cuttings, or inclined planes, or in what way the thing is to be carried into effect.

The opposition knew it had won as soon as George Stephenson left the committee room, but they laid on further punishment lest the railway men return with a new Bill the following year.

Thomas Creevey, flamboyant Whig member for Appleby, vocal opponent of almost everything proposed by reformers or technologists or liberals of any kind, acted as chief advisor and general henchman to his influential friends Lord Derby and Lord Sefton (his real father) and blustered against the railway whenever the opportunity arose. He regarded the project as 'the locomotive monster . . . navigated by a tail of smoke and sulphur, coming through every man's grounds . . .' He referred to one supporter of the Bill in committee as 'insane . . . he quite foamed at the mouth with rage . . . in support of this infernal nuisance . . .' Other canal owners railed against with similar indignation, exploiting every unconvincing claim with a solitary motive. As the contemporary economic historian Thomas Baines realised, 'with one heart and mind [they] resolved to crush the rival project, which threatened to interrupt, if not destroy, the hopes of prescription and the dreams of a sanguine avarice.'

The prospect of a railway also raised fears of social upheaval. Canal and railway navigators were saddled with a terrible criminal reputation, and their proposed presence on new land was portrayed in the worst light even by those who stood to gain by their employment. 'Possessed of all the daring recklessness of the smuggler,' wrote John Roscoe, one of the railway's earliest promoters,

their ferocious behaviour can only be equalled by the brutality of their language. It may be truly said their hand is against every man's, and before they have been long located every man's hand is against theirs. From being long known to each other they generally act in concert, and put at defiance any local constabulary force; consequently crimes of the most atrocious character were common, and robbery, without any attempt at concealment, was an everyday occurrence.

The opposition came not just from England. In the United States, one canal shareholder's protests drew the facetious attention of the *New York Gazette*. 'He saw what would be the effect of it,' the newspaper noted,

that it would set the whole world a-gadding . . . Why, you will not be able to keep an apprentice boy at his work; every Saturday evening he must take a trip to Ohio, to spend the Sabbath with his sweetheart. Grave plodding citizens will be flying about like comets. It will encourage flightiness of intellect. Various people will turn into the most immeasurable liars; all their conceptions will be exaggerated by their munificent notions of distance – 'Only a hundred miles off! Tut, nonsense, I'll step across madam and bring your fan'.

The canal man liked things how they stood – three miles an hour for express barges, two miles per hour for the rest. 'None of your hop-skip-and-jump whimsies for me.'

In the north of England, the fears were more prosaic. Cows would stop grazing, hens wouldn't lay, birds would be poisoned in the fumes, horses would become extinct. People were made to believe it would suck their very life force. Samuel Smiles, the Stephensons' first biographer, claimed that householders on the route believed their homes would burn down from the fire thrown from the locomotive chimneys, and they were worried that their crops would be unsaleable. In addition, Smiles observed that 'boilers would burst and blow passengers to atoms . . .' but also noted that the naysayers had their own consolation: 'that the weight of the locomotive would completely prevent its moving.'

Opponents of the Liverpool and Manchester line made good use of those who were involved with railways yet feared for their future. Nicholas Wood, the colliery manager at Killingworth and a friend of the Stephensons, was in general favour of locomotives, but was concerned at the hyperbole and commotion they generated. He wrote in a pamphlet in 1825:

It is far from my wish to promulgate to the world that the ridiculous expectations, or rather professions, of the enthusiastic speculist will be realised, and that we shall see engines travelling at the rate of twelve, sixteen, eighteen or twenty miles an hour. Nothing could do more harm toward their general adoption than the promulgation of such nonsense.

This was a particular feature of railways in this period: most people were forced to eat their words every couple of years.

The railway directors lost the vote on the first defining clauses of their bill and graciously withdrew it. But its failure caused only temporary dismay. Sandars, Lawrence and Booth were not men who were easily discouraged, and they had learnt much about the procedural requirements for success. Their confidence in progress was inexhaustible, and they would renew their claims within a year. In the interim they would make strategic changes to their prospectus, eradicate the key objections of their rivals, and make one significant change in their armoury: they would replace their chief engineer.

In addition, they would enlist the support of one of the two members of parliament for Liverpool, William Huskisson, who had previously expressed a genial interest in the railway project, and might be useful in ensuring its fruition.

AT THE HUSTINGS in Liverpool in 1823, Huskisson's enemies claimed he was illegitimate, but that was just dirty talk. In March 1770 he had been born within wedlock to William and Elizabeth Huskisson, a well-to-do landed couple of Staffordshire stock. One of four brothers, he grew up at Birtsmorton Court in Worcestershire, but on the death of his mother moved to the estates of his grandfather at Oxley and Bushbury, near Wolverhampton. His early education was quite as peripatetic, moving between boarding schools in Staffordshire and Leicestershire before his teens, and at both it was said that he shone at mathematics and reasoning.

At thirteen he moved again, this time abroad. His father remarried, and had further children, and Huskisson fell increasingly under the caring influence of his maternal great uncle. Dr Richard Gem, a physician with influential contacts in both politics and science, had become concerned about the prospects of the Huskisson brothers, and in 1783 he persuaded the family to let him tutor two of them – William and Richard – in the heady environs of Paris.

Dr Gem had moved there twenty years earlier to act as physician to the Duke of Bedford, Ambassador to France, and he swiftly earned one of the best medical reputations in the city. He was delighted when Richard Huskisson, William's youngest brother, exhibited keen talents in the same field, but his other charge displayed a more artistic temperament. William Huskisson read vast amounts, spoke fluent French within months, and immediately took a wide interest in the monumental social and political dramas unfolding before him. Initially at least, it was impossible to imagine a more rewarding or exciting time to be in this city of enlightenment.

Edward Leeves, Huskisson's longtime friend, wrote of how, within this period, 'fashion and philosophy had united their powers to favour the triumph of liberal opinions, and it was scarcely possible to withstand their combined influence and attractions.' France had recently emerged victorious against its greatest rival, and in helping to wrest from England its transatlantic colonies had hastened the independence of the United States. Huskisson had witnessed these events from afar, but was increasingly affected by their consequences. He met Dr Gem's friends Benjamin Franklin and Thomas Jefferson, the latter once writing to him from New York with copious thanks for his kindness while in Paris: 'I find the loss of your society and instructive conversation among the leading circumstances of regret.'

Dr Gem was a strict disciplinarian, and Huskisson found it hard to adapt to his parsimonious health regime. In an attempt to 'preserve the elasticity of the mind', Dr Gem forbade any interruptions for food during his study days, the first meal not starting until late afternoon. The young brothers both lost weight, and William reported that on one return visit to England even his family could scarcely recognise him. It took several weeks of careful nurturing before his strength was restored.

Back in Paris, Huskisson spent much spare time at the theatre, and he extolled its capacity to improve its audiences. 'The absolute liberty granted to the theatres in this kingdom will, I think, be of service to the morals of the people,' he wrote to a friend.

It is among the most striking innovations of this place to see half a dozen little stages upon the boulevards, formerly condemned to exhibit low, indecent and immoral farces, now playing the chefs d'oeuvres of Corneille,

Molliere etc. Their acting is ridiculous *to us*; but it is such as the people is accustomed to.

It was clear that he was also regularly enchanted by female actors, most of whom he would endeavour to meet. Amongst them was Lady Emma Hamilton, whose singing and acting combined for Huskisson in 'the most astonishing spectacle I ever saw', and she immediately became an object of admiration.

In his late teens, Huskisson began to take a more active political role. He witnessed the fall of the Bastille in July 1789, and keenly supported the cause of liberty and the overthrow of tyranny. He joined what was called the Club Of 1789, a reformist but moderate society concerned with supporting the monarchy within the new constitution. He also visited the anarchical Jacobin Club, an event he would later come to regret. In 1823, the year of his election in Liverpool, he was accused of revolutionary tendencies and of being a distant supporter of the vandalism and bloodshed that soaked the streets. Despite the apparent absurdity of this smear (Huskisson had been an avowed Conservative for two decades), the MP felt impelled to defend himself.

I am aware that among other calumnies which I have sometimes suffered, it has been stated that I was once an active member of the Jacobin Club. I deny that I ever belonged to that club, and I challenge any man to prove it. I never was but once in the Jacobin Club. I went there, by their permission, as other Englishmen did, to satisfy my own curiosity.

Huskisson blamed his teenage naivety; he thought the early stirrings of popular independence to be a good thing.

If, Gentlemen, it be a crime to have thought too sanguinely of mankind at the age of nineteen, and to have believed it not impossible that liberty might be sustained against despotism, without becoming the victim of anarchy, to that crime I plead guilty.

61

In the same period, at the age of twenty, he made his first significant speech, addressing the Club Of 1789 on the dangers of the proposed plan to put an enormous amount of paper money into circulation. His warning went unheeded, and the equivalent of £84 million was issued. Huskisson linked this act directly with the success of the violent revolution – 'it was the foundation of all of the subversion of property which followed' – but the clarity and conviction of his opposition was to have, if not a far-reaching effect, then at least a resounding personal one. Edward Leeves noted how

the young Englishman soon found himself an object of general interest and admiration in all the most distinguished liberal circles of that metropolis . . . his society was eagerly courted by people of the highest consideration and fashion of both sexes.

Among his new admirers was William Hayley, the biographer and poet who soon became a confidant, the painter George Romney and Dr John Warner, Chaplain at the Paris embassy. Dr Warner introduced him to his first employer, Lord Gower (later the Marquis of Stafford), for whom Huskisson became private secretary.

By June 1792 it was clear that his ardour for the revolution had cooled. In that month he wrote to William Hayley of 'the shameful and odious conduct of the people of this place,' and within three months he had fled for London. 'Scenes of horror and cruelty . . . have disgraced humanity in France and rendered its capital uninhabitable,' he wrote to Hayley in September.

The change in the government which took place on the 10th August obliged Lord Gower to return to England; the obstacles opposed to Englishmen who wished to leave Paris so great that it was almost impossible. [This] determined me to embrace the offer of returning with him to this land of true liberty.

Huskisson had been no mere observer of events. On the evening of 10 August, when it was deemed safe to walk the streets, he left his ambassadorial suite at the Hotel de Monaco to inspect the damage and gather information. But when he returned to his rooms at the hotel he found an uninvited guest. Monsieur de Champcenetz, Governor of the Tuileries, had fled his palace in fear of his life. Or rather, he jumped from a palace window once it had been stormed, and fell amongst a pile of Swiss bodies who had died trying to defend it. After lying still and undetected for several hours, he made his way to the hotel of the British Ambassador at nightfall, entered in the guise of an Englishman, and made himself comfortable at Huskisson's place until he returned and threw himself upon his mercy.

Huskisson knew de Champcenetz slightly, and realised that he was in a difficult situation. If he threw him out he would become his murderer; if he sheltered him he could embarrass the Ambassador and create a perilous situation between England and France. Keeping his guest's presence secret from Lord Gower, he hustled him out to the custody of a trustworthy laundry woman, and instructed he receive money and a safe passage. Within a week, Huskisson learnt that he had successfully escaped from Paris, and a while later that he had been returned and restored to the government of Louis XVIII.

The intensity of Huskisson's experiences in Paris established in his young mind the overriding value of constructive but moderate reform; a government had to be open to the principle of change, or be forever swept away by it. Later in his career he would plot a middle ground between extremes, and argue that 'it is the business of the statesman to move onwards with the new combinations which have grown around him.' This principle would govern his entire political life. It was entirely to his credit that, unlike many of his future parliamentary colleagues, he greeted new ideas with a measured optimism; the modern age was not something he saw fit to repel.

RICHARD TREVITHICK was born within a few months of William Huskisson in Illogan, Cornwall. His school report described him as 'a disobedient, slow, obstinate, spoiled boy, frequently absent and very inattentive,' and if he hadn't become an engineer he could have made it as a wrestler. His feats of physical showmanship were news three counties away. It was said he could tie an anvil to his thumb and lift it with ease to scratch his name on a wooden beam above his head. He liked to throw sledgehammers over the roofs of engine houses and carry heavy men across crowded rooms. He will also be remembered for making Britain's first high-pressure steam locomotives.

Trevithick worked in the local tin mines, and in the mid-1790s he joined his colleagues in a popular local challenge – how to utilise the best elements of James Watt's pumping engines without having to pay the large royalty due on his patent. This didn't expire until 1800, and applied primarily to the use of a separate condenser. Trevithick's breakthrough bypassed the need for one entirely. The first models of his high-pressure or 'strong' steam engines released the steam from the cylinder straight into the atmosphere and directed the draught through the fire-box, emitting an erratic burst of noise that gave them the name of 'puffers'. His other improvements – a cylindrical boiler and the placement of the fire-box inside its water space – ensured that far from losing pressure due to the lack of a condenser, the pumping force increased.

His lighter, faster engines were first applied to the familiar needs of water drainage and winding mechanisms. He was not the first to make a locomotive (this distinction was claimed by Nicolas Cugnot in France in 1769, a military engineer who built a road-going tricycle capable of carrying three men through the avenues of Paris until it crashed and was locked up in the nearest arsenal). But Trevithick was the first to realise their full potential by applying them to cast-iron rails and demonstrating their practical uses.

Richard Trevithick, who was always unhappy and always unlucky.

His earliest experiments were over stone and earth. With the engineering guidance of Davies Gilbert, a fellow Cornishman and future President of the Royal Society, Trevithick ran his first full-size locomotive at Camborne on Christmas Eve 1801, with one pair of wheels driven by a crank-and-axle mechanism successfully pulling a cart full of brave men up a gentle hill. James Watt's own experiments with high-pressure steam had ceased partly through his fear of explosions, and Trevithick found that these were not unfounded. His first machine was destroyed by fire as Trevithick and his friends parked it outside a hostelry, failed to shut down the engine and let its water boil away. Subsequent machines met other fates – explosions, broken axles and steering handles, public fear or disinterest – and after further attempts to drive his invention on London roads, he abandoned his efforts. From then on he concentrated on fixed engines, and built machines that could crush stone, grind corn and bore brass.

His locomotive work on rails was inspired by a wager. Two ironmasters had heard of the possibilities of these new machines, and the more optimistic, Samuel Homfray, bet his dubious colleague, Anthony Hill of Plymouth, 500 guineas that a steam locomotive could work more effectively than a horse on Homfray's local mine railway at Penydarren in South Wales. The Penydarren to Abercynon plateway stretched a little under ten miles, and in February 1804 one of Trevithick's engines drove along it hauling 10 tons of iron and five wagons holding 70 men to win the bet for Homfray. The journey took just over four hours, and Trevithick wrote to Gilbert that he could have done it in two had it not been for trees and rocks on the line. The engineer walked in front of his locomotive in a compelling show of confidence.

The Penydarren engine had coupled wheels run by a large flywheel and cogs, and although the iron track was fairly level, Trevithick used it to confront the most fundamental questions of friction and slippage, finding that the weight of the engines alone was enough to ensure good traction in fine weather. But this presented another dilemma, one that torments engineers to the present day: how to prevent the rails cracking under the colossal new load of moving machines.

His most popular locomotive, Catch Me Who Can, was set up in 1808 on a circular track encased by high wooden walls on desolate land not far from what was to become London's Euston Station, and was announced on its tickets as 'Mechanical Power Subduing Animal Speed'; ever the showman, Trevithick claimed his engine could outrun any horse at Newmarket. It cost one shilling to view and ride behind it, and attracted thousands of nervous visitors, but the track had to be continually replaced and Trevithick became disillusioned with its prospects and his failure to attract new investment. It was the last locomotive he attempted, and he was to be marked as a visionary but impetuous man. The *Civil Engineer* and *Architect's Journal* concluded that he was 'always unhappy and always unlucky; always beginning something new and never ending what he had in hand.' But his importance did not go unnoticed in the north of England; the essential principle of his last engine – a boiler piston driving a horizontal bar which was attached by rods to the wheels – was still apparent in locomotive design twenty years later.

Catch Me Who Can: magnificent circles in 1808.

THE LOCOMOTIVE DEVELOPMENTS of the intervening years came directly from the mines, a parade of fascinating contraptions and dazzling ingenuity. In 1811, John Blenkinsop, the co-owner of Middleton Colliery in Leeds, commissioned the engineer Matthew Murray to build a dual-cylindered, six-wheeled locomotive with its central pair cogged against lugs on the outside of the track. It succeeded in preventing wheel slippage, and hauled heavy loads in cumbersome fashion, but was quite unsuited to speedy traffic. The same conclusion was reached after a demonstration of William Brunton's Mechanical Traveller, which drove itself with the aid of two iron legs between its wheels at the back. Another novel machine, the Grasshopper, was the first locomotive to appear at the Wylam colliery on the north bank of the Tyne, its name derived from the alternating beams above its boiler. Its best features were incorporated in 1815 in a new engine designed by William Hedley, the colliery's mechanical inspector. Puffing Billy was intended to replace the horses dragging coal to the river's edge, but it took a year of alterations to its boiler and complex overhead linkages to create enough pressure to propel its wheels via gears and axles. But Hedley did succeed in demonstrating that no cogging system was required even on tracks with mild gradients, and his elaborate engine – resembling something closer to a cotton spinning machine than anything that had yet been seen on a rail – came to the attention of the thirty-four-year-old George Stephenson, who had grown up on the route of the Wylam Colliery wagonway, and had witnessed – heard, smelt, choked upon – each development of track and drag upon it. He had just begun to make engines of his own.

* * *

FROM 1790, the year in which he lost his father, Huskisson was keenly aware of the importance of maintaining his own good health. At the age of twenty he wrote to his friend William Hayley in praise of his latest purchase, 'for I am persuaded that bathing is one of the most powerful remedies for shattered health and those frequent aberrations from our original gaiety which are the consequences of it.'

Puffing Billy, at work 40 years after its first appearance.

Huskisson corresponded with Hayley about once a fortnight, and his letters contain a candour not seen elsewhere in his writings. Almost all his letters to him begin '*Mon très cher Pere*', and within the text he occasionally addresses him as Father. In response, Hayley begins his letters '*Mon Très Cher Fils*'. Their correspondence was Huskisson's principal outlet for his emotions at this time, and he would express his frustration with his work and health. Even the mildest ailments were addressed.

I am upon the whole better, having nearly succeeded in getting rid of my cough. [I] am now what I must be content hereafter to call well; c'est a dire, my former healthy disposition changed into an enfeebled habit . . . without having however to complain of the existence of any real illness.

In 1794 he recorded 'a little shock from an attack of the dysentery now so prevalent. The principal symptom of the complaint, thank God, has left me, and now I only feel weakness, and a little remains of the fever which accompanied it.'

Huskisson's reputation for frailty at such a young age was apparently not confined to his closest friends. Dealing with his father's estate papers in Staffordshire, he found that solicitors were using his past weaknesses as an excuse for the great delays in the legal procedures. He came across a document in which he was astonished to find that he apparently was unable 'to undertake a journey to London without the most imminent personal danger . . .' He wrote to Hayley that 'I cannot forbear laughing at its nonsense.'

But sometimes he was his own worst enemy. Referring to the prospects of a new secretarial job, he feared only the side-effects:

I shall certainly exert myself to show that I am worthy of it, not without regretting sometimes that these efforts will deprive me of many happy hours, and contribute still more to injure my health.

These constant considerations of his well-being were not uncommon for the times, and were enhanced in Huskisson's case by the vivid tales relayed to him by his brother Richard, who, under Dr Gem's guidance, did become a doctor. He worked predominantly abroad as a medical naval officer, travelling to St Helena on a frigate in 1793. Another ship also sailed that year, losing almost seventy of its crew to scurvy and other diseases, while William Huskisson noted in correspondence that his brother's ship returned without losing a single man. This he attributed to his brother alone. 'His principal care was not to administer a few ineffectual drugs, until the death of his patient relieved him from his task, but to watch, and guard against, the causes of the complaint.' Richard Huskisson then travelled to Barbados upon crowded troop ships, educating the men as best he could, and going from bunk to bunk administering medicines when disease took hold. His brother described great valour. 'Exposed [to disease], as he was by this conduct, he escaped the infection much longer than most of those who, from fear, forsook their duty.'

But he succumbed eventually. Indeed, the early 1790s was a time of sustained personal grief for Huskisson. Four years after the death of his father at the age of forty-seven, his youngest brother Richard died at the age of twenty-three. 'I have now been suffering for three weeks with the severest pangs of mental distress,' he wrote to Hayley in August 1794, a letter sealed with black wax.

My health not a little deranged, has not permitted me sooner to make known to you afresh . . . My Brother is no more. A general officer, whose acquaintance he could scarcely be said to enjoy, writes from Guadeloupe to my friend Mr Nepean. 'We have lost a young man of the most extraordinary abilities, victim of his professional zeal . . .' I can dwell no longer, my dear Father, on this heart-rending subject . . .

This letter was swiftly followed by another. 'So soon after our first separation in life,' he wrote to Hayley,

I am thus deprived of the companion of my infancy, of my education, and of almost every hour of my existence. However long [my life] may be, I feel that the best half of it is gone.'

He asked his friend to write a loving verse for a marble memorial. In part it reads:

> Brave, sensible, humane, thy mind and heart
> Completely fashioned for the healing art,
> Led thee, young Huskisson, with guardian care
> To rescue valour from perdition's snare:
> Teaching the mariner, in noxious seas,
> To foil the hovering harpy of disease:
> Thy bolder piety laboured to sustain
> The soldier drooping with contagious pain . . .
> A brother who in thee could once rejoice,

(His bosom friend by nature and by choice)
Feels and records on this thy vacant tomb
Pride in thy work, and anguish in thy doom.

(Hayley would later be remembered principally as a benefactor of William Blake; certainly his verse was frowned upon, Robert Southey famously writing that 'Everything about that man is good except his poetry'.)

BY 1795, at the age of twenty-five, William Huskisson's political career had begun. On his return from France he continued to spend time with Lord Gower, and at his residence in London frequently met the Prime Minister, William Pitt, and Henry Dundas, MP for Edinburgh and Treasurer of the Navy. Over dinner one evening, Lord Gower told Pitt and Dundas of a letter he had received from a French woman seeking entry to England, one of hundreds of similar requests from those desperate to flee the new regime. Many had already arrived without papers. Dundas believed that the claims of the emigrés should be handled by someone fluent in the language and the business of diplomatic protocol, and Huskisson was immediately selected for such a role. As it was described to him, his job was

to show every possible civility and respect to all foreigners, whose conduct in this country had not given rise to any suspicion, and especially to save to the ladies the trouble of appearing at the public offices.

Huskisson took the night to consider the opportunity, and accepted it in the morning. He was right to be wary: it entailed only rather miserable administration, and took up every waking hour; he had previously spent little time in London, but now found no time to enjoy what it offered. He sold his father's Staffordshire estate in 1794, a sum that brought him £13,000, rising to almost double this following the death of his brother and a distant elderly relative, and he now considered himself an independent and metropolitan soul free of almost all of his family's traditional landed ties and duties.

There was no concealing his ambitions or his distress with his present employment, or in the job that followed. In 1795 he was appointed as assistant to Evan Nepean, the Under-Secretary of State for War and the Colonies, where his days were spent transcribing letters regarding the procurement of army supplies for overseas troops. In a familiar pattern for Huskisson, his days were punctuated by poor health. 'I am daily undergoing so much fatigue both in mind and body which in my present state I am but ill able to bear,' he wrote to Hayley.

Nepean, who on every occasion has shown himself so friendly to me, has been confined to his bed [for three weeks] with a most excruciating rheumatism, which has taken fast hold of every part of his body, and is attended with a violent fever. His life has been twice despaired of, and he now lies in a very precarious situation, and so sore that he cannot bear the bedclothes on any part of him. The whole of his official duties, in addition to my own, have fallen to me.

Following his recovery, Nepean was promoted to Secretary of the Admiralty, and Pitt appointed Huskisson his successor. He wasn't delighted. 'Would it be wise in me to throw away the best years of my life in the migratory and contemptible occupation of a Chief Clerk?' he asked Nepean, whose friendship he believed could withstand such honesty.

To return every day to a post which would keep alive my present sensations makes me despicable whilst I held it, and unfit for real business when called to a better, to which I might then prove a disgrace.

His letter to Nepean was a plea for influence, for it concluded: 'If a seat in Parliament was added as soon as an opportunity offered,

I should be gratified in the greatest object of my ambition.' Just such an opportunity arose towards the end of 1796, when a seat became vacant in Morpeth, a small market town midway between Newcastle-upon-Tyne and the Scottish Borders. At first, Huskisson showed little talent for the job, and it was eighteen months before he delivered his maiden speech. His Tory friends assigned his nervousness to his youth – he was still only twenty-seven. But his Whig opponents claimed he was one of the most inadequate public speakers they had ever heard.

HUSKISSON'S UNCLE died in Paris in 1800. Dr Gem bequeathed to his nephew his estate in Worcestershire; in time other property evolved to him including a mortgage on the Eartham estate in Sussex, which soon became his new home.

On learning of Dr Gem's death, Huskisson wrote that he believed 'he would have found in my present situation much that would have been gratifying to his affection.' In truth, Huskisson's present situation was marked primarily by a numbing and obsequious devotion to duty. His early political career contained few moments of clarity or sparkle, being instead weighed down with the sort of laborious administration that inevitably afflicted all undersecretaries.

His friend Edward Leeves suggested that Huskisson realised the limitations of his oratory, and remained in awe of those who were able to hold the attention of an audience by their strength of character alone. Huskisson also noted that his colleagues often received a little chemical boost to their public endeavours: at a dinner attended by Lord Broughton, Huskisson surprised his guests with an unusual observation on Lord Liverpool and the austere Lord Castlereagh: 'Both took ether, as an excitement, before speaking.'

But Huskisson's 'ascent to the Temple of Fame' was marked by dogged patience. He remained at the department for War and the Colonies until 1801, when he resigned alongside his great influences Pitt and George Canning. He returned to Parliament three years later as representative of the port city of Liskeard, and in 1806, following the death of Pitt, as member for Harwich.

Huskisson became Secretary to the Treasury, where his singular achievement was defining a new relationship between the Treasury and the Bank of England. Writing in 1831, Edward Leeves observed that even when in full command of his subject, Huskisson 'seemed reluctant to give the reins to his imagination, and studiously to draw back, as though trenching on forbidden ground.' Partly this was attributed to the 'constitutional diffidence' he had held since boyhood, but there was another reason also. His friend Canning was a far more eloquent speaker, and Huskisson was content to sublimate his own ambitions beneath those of a colleague with whom he agreed on almost every issue. 'Huskisson's was the way, not of glittering phrase and momentary triumph, but of logical argument and facts skilfully marshalled, and his aim not facile persuasion but lasting conviction,' Liverpool's historian George Veitch concluded in a paper delivered to the Historic Society of Lancashire and Cheshire in 1929.

Canning had the restless, intriguing mind, self-torturing yet a torment to his fellows, which is the bane of the imaginative politician. Huskisson had that profound loyalty which moves a few rare spirits, well knowing the cost, to make sacrifices for their friends, and to merge their own accomplishments in the triumph of another.

By 1810, the Canningites – primarily Canning himself, Huskisson and Sturges Bourne – had formed a recognisable new wing of the Tory party. Drawing inspiration directly from the younger Pitt, Liberal Toryism stood in direct contrast to the arch High Toryism of their elders. Favouring Catholic emancipation and steady economic reform, their enlightenment was best described by Burke as 'the disposition to preserve and the ability to improve taken together;' or as the Whig Lord Brougham saw it, 'Canning's principles were above the prejudices of the bigots who have rendered Toryism ridiculous.'

The Canningites drew their support principally from the new middle classes, whereas the High Tories relied on the more prominent influences of Church and landed interests. The historian Alexander Brady noted precisely a century after Huskisson's death that no one represented the staunch views of traditional Toryism better than Lord Eldon, who believed that political health demanded only political immobility. Eldon denied concessions to the demands of reform 'on the ground that such concessions, instead of satisfying existing needs, created further demands.'

It was Huskisson's allegiance to Canning that, more than any other judgement, led to the stunting of a potentially brilliant career, frequently casting him in muted opposition even when his own party was in power. But such a situation would prove useful to certain external forces gathering momentum beyond the gates of Parliament. To several figures in the north of England, Huskisson's unique position – an independent mind in a nervous administration – would prove a decisive tool in the development of an exciting new form of public transportation.

L ONG BEFORE HE BECAME ITS MP, Huskisson's connection with the mercantile interests of Liverpool was already advanced. In the election of 1812, he was persuaded to stand as member for Chichester (he lived six miles away on his estate at Eartham), and he was elected unopposed. He found it one of the less corrupt electoral areas of the day, and his representation of the community's commercial concerns earned widespread respect for a decade; the lack of warmth for which he was often associated in the House of Commons was not in evidence as he strolled the Cathedral City.

He was, in fact, often absent from Chichester. For several months in 1814 Huskisson journeyed back and forth to Liverpool, a venture that would take almost a day by coach and horses. Canning had been elected one of the two MPs for Liverpool in 1812, but when he briefly became Ambassador to Lisbon he asked Huskisson to look after the city's business in his absence. So began a rewarding relationship that would last until his death.

It is hard today to overestimate the importance of Liverpool's ports to Britain's trade at the beginning of the nineteenth century, and as hard to overstate the significance of Liverpool's representation at Westminster. Leeds, Manchester and Birmingham returned no members to Parliament, despite their newfound importance in the industrial and technological revolutions. Liverpool, an ancient borough, returned two, and their election was keenly fought on relatively principled grounds. In 1812 Canning and the traditional Tory General Isaac Gascoyne stood against the Whig pairing of Thomas Creevey and Henry Brougham, and the poll amongst 2,726 eligible voters decided narrowly for the two Tories. Huskisson's responsibilities in Canning's absence were largely fiscal and commercial, and he juggled these with his lucrative new appointment as Colonial Agent to Ceylon. He seemed to spend much time at the dockside: he received the eternal gratitude of local merchants Ince, Drinkwater, Carson and Parry for retrieving their tea and coffee imports from the Revenue; and from the merchant John Tobin, on whose behalf Huskisson appealed to the Treasury for remuneration after one of his ships was 'condemned', possibly amid accusations of smuggling. Henceforth Drinkwater would become Liverpool's mayor, and Tobin would become a lifelong friend; sixteen years later it would be Sir John who would accompany Huskisson and his wife to the opening of the railway.

Huskisson's own election as a representative of Liverpool in 1823 was described in the influential Tory journal *Fraser's Magazine* as succeeding 'merely on the ground of his political talents and standing, without any of the usual inducements.' Initially he was reluctant to take Canning's place, complaining he could not 'cast off Chichester as I would an old shoe'. He was eventually persuaded by the additional bearing of Sir John Gladstones, a prominent and wealthy local merchant who had become friendly with Huskisson in 1814 and understood the importance of having a progressive local representative of his shipping interests (he owned plantations in the West Indies and the United States). Gladstone – he dropped the 's' in his name to ease pronunciation – had initially wooed Canning to Liverpool a decade before, and it was with Canning's help that Gladstone himself became an MP in 1818. When Gladstone lost his seat in 1827, it was amidst accusations of bribery.

Huskisson's election was assured but not uncontested. Typically, the frail candidate feared for his health in the campaign to come, writing to his wife from the hustings that he was 'now wishing heartily' that he had remained in Chichester, 'instead of having the battle to fight here.' He was accused of being an 'alien' on account of his upbringing in France, and even an illegitimate one. But a subsequent post brought Mrs Huskisson a report from one of her husband's backers that everyone was surprised how warmly and vividly he spoke to his audience, and how they 'have been won as much by the manliness with which he has avowed his principles, as by the conciliatoriness and prudence of his manner and conduct.' Huskisson remained daunted by the amount of speeches he was obliged to deliver and by the public meetings he should attend, and was no doubt relieved when Gladstone informed him that he had reduced both amounts dramatically 'by a little management'.

On 14 February 1823, Huskisson was declared victorious by 236 votes to 31, the poll closing hours early once the outcome was certain. He was then carried through the streets from the Town Hall to a reception hosted by the merchant John Bolton and Gladstone. Gladstone had his child in tow, a thirteen-year-old boy called William Ewart. There was no doubting Sir John's ambitions, both for his son and himself; by drawing Huskisson into his web, his ambitions took a step forward. Ever keen to increase his influence and commercial routes, Gladstone told his new Member of Parliament that he was already excited by a scheme being proposed by his friend Joseph Sandars that would one day link Liverpool and Manchester by rail.

IN JUNE 1823 a new firm called Robert Stephenson and Co. was established primarily to manufacture steam engines, although it would be several years before it was clear whether fixed or travelling machines would make up the bulk of their orders. Its directors made up the perfect blend of experience and young enthusiasm – George Stephenson, his nineteen-year-old son Robert, Michael Longridge (manager of the Bedlington Iron Works) and Edward Pease (of the Stockton and Darlington). Or such was the plan: Robert Stephenson left his studies at Edinburgh University to become the managing partner, and spent the first few months travelling to London and beyond with his father to gather orders. Their first commissions were boilers and mill pumps, but their biggest orders, for four large stationary winding engines, came from the Stockton and Darlington Railway. But Robert Stephenson seemed restless with his new engagement, unhappy that his own ambition to improve existing engines and design new ones was overshadowed by the needs of company management and his father's own prowess. Only a few months after the firm was founded he accepted what he hoped would be a more fulfilling challenge working for another company in Colombia. His departure caused Michael Longridge much unease, but he wasted little time in hiring two replacements: James Kennedy, a respected marine engineer, and Timothy Hackworth, a former foreman blacksmith alongside William Hedley at Wylam Colliery. Hackworth was a deeply religious father of eight whose Methodist beliefs led to his departure from Wylam when he refused to work on Sundays. But he was a gifted young engineer who had submitted locomotive designs for the Stockton and Darlington line, and Stephenson & Co. was happy to have him briefly as a partner rather than competitor.

The company was originally based at Longridge's Bedlington Iron Works, but by 1824 it was firmly established with its own smith's shop in large new premises in South Street in the west end of Newcastle, within an area known as Forth Street. George Stephenson was rarely present, but his skills appeared to have been exploited everywhere else. In the first few years, eager for any business, the company accepted a wide variety of manufacturing orders, from boilers for collieries and ships to paper-making machinery. But George Stephenson's passion was always for the railways, and it would be his skill as a surveyor and consultant engineer for almost every new major railway project under consideration that would ensure the success of his engine works. Despite even the most rigorous efforts by railway directors throughout the country to ensure they obtained the best equipment at the cheapest price, the Stephensons' monopoly of expertise and influence ensured that only perverseness would prevent new orders for railway goods coming to them. Stephenson had established his reputation at Killingworth Colliery with his lumbering but powerful engines that made modest improvements on the work of Trevithick and Hedley, but his ambitions had gradually widened to encompass all aspects of railway design and fitting. Not long after the opening of the Stockton and Darlington line in September 1825, Stephenson was supervising and supplying equipment for the Canterbury and Whitstable line, the Nantlle Railway in North Wales, and the Monkland and Kirkintilloch Railway in Scotland, his company providing wagons, wheels, chairs and stationary engines that would haul goods by rope. There can be no mistaking his pride in aggrandisement when he noted in a letter that 'The Bolton and Leigh Railway has again fallen into my hands . . .' or when he spotted a newspaper advertisement placed by another company's directors for the supply of wheels and axles: 'I have no doubt I shall get them to manufacture at my place . . .'

Huskisson and Canning, who couldn't do without each other.

IN WESTMINSTER there was also a distinct spirit of progress. Lord Castlereagh's suicide in August 1822 was caused by his fear of an impending homosexual sex scandal, but his emotional instability may also have stemmed from excessive pressures of work. Lord Liverpool, the century's longest-serving prime minister with an unbroken period of office between 1812 and 1827, had come to rely on Castlereagh for much of his party's direction, first overseas and then at home (indeed Liverpool was often regarded as a mere cipher, an arch-mediocrity). Castlereagh's death resulted in a reshuffle of his cabinet and a significant shift in policy. The coldness and austerity that marked Castlereagh's tenure would gradually be replaced by a more refreshing Liberal breeze; Huskisson's and Canning's time had come at last.

Huskisson was introduced to the Cabinet in 1823 as President of the Board of Trade and Treasurer of the Navy; Canning became Foreign Secretary and then Chancellor. Their friendship guaranteed their influence and bound their fate; Canning's death in 1827 would greatly restrict Huskisson's advance. Their relationship was well summarised by *Fraser's Magazine*:

Mr Canning had all the airs and graces that could demand a debating club. No man surpassed him in a fine flow of excellent words, which took their places with a most wonderful degree of order, considering their quantity, and the uselessness of so many of the number . . . He was, therefore, the light of his section; but all brilliancy would not do, and Huskisson was the shade. Mr Canning determined that as he was to be the wit, somebody else was to be the philosopher; and Huskisson was the man.

Huskisson's career now pursued an alliterative three-way course: currency, commerce and colonies. His position on the major reforms of the day – the Corn Laws and free trade, Catholic emancipation and parliamentary reform – would lead him to be regarded as enlightened, far-sighted, realistic, misguided and dangerous, but even his opponents respected him for the integrity and consistency of his beliefs, and for the intelligence of his arguments. In his memoirs, Lord Greville found Huskisson 'tall, slouchy and ignoble looking' as well as

extremely agreeable, without much animation, generally cheerful, with a great deal of humour, information and anecdote, gentlemanlike, unassuming, slow in speech, and with a downcast look, as if he avoided meeting anybody's gaze.

His conclusion was unequivocal. 'It is probably true that there is no man in Parliament or perhaps out of it, so well versed in finance, commerce, trade and colonial matters.'

Not long after his entry to the cabinet, Huskisson was again hampered by illness. He caught the flu with preposterous regularity. 'I regret very much to say that I am positively enjoined not to venture at all out of doors till the severity of the weather shall abate,' he began a letter to Canning at a crucial period of the discussion over the Corn Laws.

I have seen none of my colleagues today, and have had no opportunity of communicating to any of them the facility which exists of postponing Corn from Monday to Thursday . . . I am too much exhausted to enter upon any other topic, and I am afraid that you will find ample proof that I am so in what I have already written.

In retrospect, Huskisson seems to have been an unlikely early supporter of the Corn Law of 1815, an act which embodied many of the protectionist principles which he later rallied against. The domestic corn industry was suffering from lower-priced imports, and Huskisson had argued that 'to ensure a continuance of cheapness and sufficiency, we must ensure our own growers . . . protection against foreign import'. The new law prohibited the entry of overseas corn until the British price reached 80 shillings a quarter; the corresponding restriction on wheat was set at 67 shillings. It was a deeply unpopular act, dramatically increasing the price of basic foods. The landed interest in Parliament, which hoped the law would remedy a dramatic loss of income in the previous years, faced not only popular opposition in the streets, but also great pressure from economists and social reformers to abolish or amend the act. And William Cobbett was to be proved right in his argument that the improvements in the price of corn would not be sustained.

The influential economist David Ricardo would soon convince Huskisson of the need for reform, and a decade later Huskisson's views on restrictive practices had undergone a complete turnaround. One speech he delivered in Liverpool in the mid-1820s caused a huge political rumpus, not least because he was reported as saying, 'the whole question is settled, and the trade in corn is to be free, and corn is hereafter to be admitted upon a duty to the great benefit of the shipowners and the trading part of the community in general.'

In the face of great political opposition from his own party, especially the Duke of Wellington, Huskisson argued that he had been misquoted and had never claimed repeal as a fait accompli, but by then his sympathies were clear. His support for free trade throughout the 1820s was unswerving, and would win him many opponents (the Corn Law would undergo several modifications in the next twenty years, though complete repeal would not come until 1846). Although he never publicly aligned himself with the social and utilitarian reforms advocated by Jeremy Bentham and John Stuart Mill, and while he always maintained great pride in Empire, his broad doctrine of liberality and laissez faire marked him as one of the most progressive members of the government. To the landowning ultra Tories this made him a dangerous man.

The mercantile debates of the 1820s coincided with a period of great public distress, a condition which Huskisson himself was blamed for bringing about. His free trade doctrine was inextricably bound up with what had become known as the currency problem, a problem with a twenty-two-year history. In 1797 the Bank of England had suspended cash payments due to a shortage of coin and bullion brought on by the public fear of foreign invasion. It was intended as a temporary measure, but the Government found it so beneficial, not least during a period of war, that the suspension remained for more than two decades. The side-effects were predictable, as the large expansion in the amount of notes in circulation brought on rapid inflation. Then the opposite occurred: because the paper currency was not immediately convertible, Britain suffered from a severe fall in foreign exchange and a rise in the cost of bullion in terms of the existing currency. In 1810, the market price for gold was 15 per cent above the mint price; promissory notes could no longer be cashed in for the full amount printed upon them. The decrease in the amount of currency caused the failure of hundreds of country banks.

Huskisson's years at the Treasury had led him to side with Ricardo in the belief that the country was being ruined by an excessive issue of banknotes, and advocated a return to the gold standard to ensure stability and guaranteed exchange rates. In 1810 he wrote an influential pamphlet outlining how the supply of precious metals underpinned the value of circulating currency, and how a stable currency benefited foreign trade.

Huskisson's actions would be vindicated in the long term, but the return to gold in 1810 was at least partially responsible for a great reduction in rural wages (a 35 per cent fall from 1819 to 1822, far more than Huskisson had predicted), and the protests that accompanied this fall mingled with other popular pressures, not least a repeal of the Corn Law and the movement to extend the franchise to the new industrial centres. The climax had been witnessed at Peterloo. According to the Birmingham banker Thomas Attwood, Huskisson's deflationary policies had amplified the unrest, indeed 'had created more misery, more poverty, more discord, more of everything that was calamitous to the nation, except death, than Attila caused in the Roman Empire.'

Huskisson pushed on undaunted. In the mid-1820s, a time of unusually prolonged health at the Board of Trade, Huskisson entered his most productive period. With the guidance of James Hume, his assistant joint secretary, his economic policy contained a consistency and reforming zeal not seen in his predecessors', and he pushed through the abolition of customs duties, the trade barriers between Britain and Ireland, reformed the Navigation Acts which had previously shackled the British colonies to the strictest of mercantile regulations, eased the restrictions on Scottish linen manufacturers and consolidated over eighty old revenue laws into eleven new Acts. There were social and industrial reforms as well, with Huskisson campaigning for an act to improve the relations between employers and their workers and for the repeal of the Combination Acts, the measures which had prohibited any gathering of people to improve their lot.

This period inspired Huskisson to his most vigorous eloquence. In one speech, concerning the benefits that free trade would bring to the silk industry, he used Spain as a prime lesson in what happened to a country that did not modernise its commercial and mercantile practice. In Spain, 'restriction has been added to restriction', leading to

the most perfect model of fallen greatness and internal misery . . . an example to be traced not only in the annihilation of her commerce and maritime power, but in her scanty revenue, her bankrupt resources, in the wretchedness of her population, and in her utter insignificance among the great powers of the world.

Huskisson greatly reduced and simplified import duties on linen, on printed books, and on glass. But he was particularly concerned with the duties on metals. He cut the duty on raw copper from £54 to £27 a ton, on zinc from £28 to £14 a ton, and on tin from £5 9s 3d to £2 10s a cwt. Then there was the question of iron. This had a levy of £6 10s a ton, a figure which greatly limited the import of cheaper and often superior iron from Sweden. He cut the duty to £1 10s a ton, ensuring not only an influx of cheaper raw iron but greater competition and efficiency among British manufacturers. The influence on the continued development of industry would be considerable, and the influence on the new railways would be immense.

Two days after Huskisson had given a typical speech in the Commons advocating a reduction in excise duties on brandy, whisky, copper and brass – 'nothing could be so visionary as to suppose that the Government might with safety . . . remit all the duties upon every article which had a tendency to encourage smuggling' – he turned his attention to a closely related matter, though the title of the new debate appeared quite unconnected: the Liverpool and Manchester Railway Bill.

CHARLES BLACKER VIGNOLES, a slender Irishman of barely nine stone, features only fleetingly in Booth and Walker's pamphlets and the newspaper accounts of the making of the railway. In truth, alongside Sandars and James, he had one of the strongest claims on its success. Vignoles was the man who surveyed what became, to all practical purposes, the final route of the line, and the person who finally sweet-talked it through Parliament. Unfortunately for Vignoles and his reputation, he also developed the fiercest of enemies in George Stephenson.

He was born in County Wexford in 1793, and was orphaned as an infant. He trained as a military officer at Sandhurst, but found that his skills lay outdoors, and he developed a passion for exploration and travel writing. He was an extravagant man, and to pay off his debts and maintain a young family he was attracted abroad to make maps and surveys. In 1822 he wrote a popular book about the Florida coast and landscape, but most of his goals went unrealised,

Charles Blacker Vignoles, who sought revenge.

and he was defrauded of much money owed to him for his important surveys of Charleston and the Florida Keys. In April 1823 he booked his return passage to England, and henceforth his luck improved.

In London, Vignoles's career took another deviation, and he found work as an assistant engineer on the docks in Bermondsey.

Here he designed his first bridge, followed by the first suspension bridge at Hammersmith, and his tutors were impressed by his energy, and by his ability to learn the newest drafting and structural techniques. Within a year he had his own business and was dining with Thomas Telford and Marc Isambard Brunel, the titans of bridge and tunnel construction. He obtained work on southern docks and rivers, and a survey of waterways in the fens brought him into contact with the engineers John and George Rennie, principally famous for their construction of Waterloo and London Bridge.

Towards the end of 1824 the Rennies had been retained for another groundbreaking project: a survey for a railway between London and Brighton. The Rennies engaged Vignoles to complete a study of gradients and costs within four weeks, and although he had never worked on such a project before, his route was the one adopted with very little amendment some years later. But it was his next survey that was to provide him most satisfaction and ultimate grief. In July 1825, John and George Rennie received a request from Joseph Sandars and Charles Lawrence: would they be willing to switch their attentions to the most ambitious railway-building proposal in the country?

WHEN THE DIRECTORS of the Liverpool and Manchester Railway parted company with George Stephenson after his calamitous performance at Westminster, Joseph Sandars gave him vague assurances that he would one day return to Liverpool. He bided his time by planning smaller routes and celebrating the opening of the Stockton and Darlington line. The railway opened on 27 September 1825, and Edward Pease later recalled how the scene on that first morning 'sets description at defiance'. A vast crowd cheered, and 'the happy faces of many, the vacant stare of astonishment of others, and the alarm depicted on the countenances of some, gave variety to the picture.'

The Stockton and Darlington . . .

Stephenson drove a locomotive built by his own firm in Newcastle. Locomotion (or 'No. 1 Travelling Engine' as it was still called by its makers) had a familiar 'grasshopper' parallel motion and initially ran behind a horseman clearing the path with a flag, but Stephenson became impatient and ordered him away so that he might reach 15 miles an hour. One contemporary report counted a procession of thirty-eight trucks not including the engine, a mixture of coal wagons drawn by locomotive and impromptu passenger wagons drawn by horse. 'Nothing could exceed the beauty and grandeur of the scene,' one observer noted. 'Throughout the whole distance, the fields and lanes were covered with elegantly-dressed females, and all descriptions of spectators.' Musicians from the small town of Yarm joined for the run between Darlington and Stockton, on its way to a banquet at the Town Hall and twenty-three boisterous toasts.

. . . and the No. 1 Engine: a vision of the future.

In time, Stephenson found a reliable way of turning the Stockton
and Darlington from a system of transporting coal into one that also
carried passengers. This had always been his intention, although on
the opening day there was only one official passenger coach (and
this for the railway's directors). He was dismayed by the hundreds
of people who ignored safety warnings and had crammed themselves into the coal wagons, jumping on at several breaks in the journey and hanging on to the sides. It was apparent that the railway was
just too forceful and novel an invention to be governed by decorum
or common sense – no rules were big enough to hold it.

In the following months, passenger travel proved a great local
diversion and a huge commercial success, operated not by the railway company but by local road carriers. People would journey from
afar to sit on the open wagons and be taken somewhere on smooth

gentle rails, even if they had nothing to do when they got there but come back. But their primitive coaches were only rarely drawn by those wheezing steam boilers, for they were judged both dangerous and unreliable; it was still mostly horses that took the strain.

At Westminster, the success of the Stockton and Darlington line was hailed by the Liverpool men as proof that a railway did not disturb the stability of the constitution, but they kept its chief architect out of sight. The Rennies presented the more refined model of the modern engineer, their London tongue and impressive construction record already an advantage over the bluff and distant achievements of Stephenson before they even began work. The Rennies knew the Duke of Wellington and had their own friends in the Commons, and there was no one better placed to commit a second application to Parliament.

Sandars and his colleagues knew little about Charles Vignoles, whom the Rennies had swiftly appointed their chief surveyor, but he too fitted the requirements: he was suave, diplomatic and very eager to please, and unlike Stephenson he had no great aspirations elsewhere.

George Rennie and Vignoles spent the summer of 1825 on horseback, making critical changes to the surveys of James and Stephenson. Their route took a more southerly course, and it was skilfully designed to bypass much of its opponents' land and throw off many of the complaints that had dogged its passage a few weeks before. The line took a more direct route, shortening its length from 33 miles to 30 and three-quarters. It avoided the awkward northward path out of Liverpool towards Bootle, just as it avoided the towns of St Helens, where local opposition was fiercest. The line headed due east, towards Walton, and from there through Childwall, Huyton, Prescot, Warrington, Leigh, and Eccles. As much of the opposition had focussed on the disruption to the streets of the main towns, the new route terminated outside Manchester at Salford, and avoided the roads of Liverpool by the proposed construction of a tunnel beneath the town stretching 2,200 feet, and a cutting through two miles of solid rock at one end of the tunnel at Olive Mount. The route required two other spectacular feats: two steep inclines to get the railway coaches over both sides of Rainhill, and a way of getting the locomotives safely over that immense quagmire at Chat Moss.

Rennie and Vignoles employed seven assistants, and again conducted much work by torchlight. One evening they achieved a significant breakthrough. Their first encounter with Captain Robert Bradshaw MP, the Duke of Bridgewater's canal manager, was far less of an ordeal than they had anticipated. 'Mr Bradshaw had contrived to earn for himself a terrible name for severity,' Vignoles noted, 'but I found him a gentleman.' There was no evidence that his opposition to the railway was weakening – he initially accused Vignoles of poaching and trespass – but he may have come to accept its inevitability. He did at least have a working relationship with Vignoles and Rennie, and Vignoles claimed that it was the start of a process that would eventually see the Marquis of Stafford, a principal shareholder in the Bridgewater canal, soften his own opposition.

The new survey submitted by Vignoles at the close of 1825 contained one detail that leapt out above the others: the estimated cost of construction had risen from £400,000 to £510,000. To accommodate this, the Railway Company favoured one practical solution and offered a principal shareholding to Robert Bradshaw. The thinking was simple: the proprietors of the Duke of Bridgewater's Canal could offset what they perceived as the financial damage to their business by profiting from the cause of their loss. Bradshaw declined the offer, but it was soon accepted by the Marquis of Stafford, who took out 1,000 shares at £100 each, a deal which also gave him the right to appoint three directors to the railway board. The deal instantly dismissed all claims from one of the railway's great adversaries.

The second Liverpool and Manchester Railway Bill was set in motion only three days after the defeat of the first. Joseph Sandars and his friends called a meeting at the Royal Hotel in London for those MPs who shared their progressive outlook. Twenty-one members showed themselves, and they resolved to try again. One of them produced a fresh expert opinion, which stated that it would indeed be possible to run a rail over even the softest marshland, given the right preparation. William Huskisson proposed a motion that reiterated the need for improved transport between Liverpool and Manchester, and said that he perceived nothing in the rejection of the Bill that should deter the subscribers from renewing their application. Henry Booth, who was present at the meeting, noted that Huskisson

considered the measure under discussion of great public importance; and whatever temporary opposition it might meet, he conceived that Parliament must ultimately give its sanction to the undertaking.

A new prospectus, submitted with the petition for the second Bill in February 1826, contained a few important changes to the first. It began with claims that it had rectified all the key faults of the first submission, and could now discharge all the objections raised against it. Its new route upset fewer men. Its new engineers were more skilful. The new attitude towards the steam locomotive was less enthusiastic: at this stage, the railway proprietors stated, they were not looking for any clause empowering them to use locomotives of any sort, and if they were permitted to use them, they would comply with any stipulations that Parliament might impose. This pained Charles Vignoles in particular, an avid supporter of engines he had seen at the collieries, but he was told to bite his lip for political gain.

The prospectus then reaffirmed its previous arguments, which had also improved: the amount of goods passing between Liverpool and Manchester had continued to increase; the advantage to passengers wishing to travel on the line was proposed keenly for the first time; and it was again contested that England's standing in the world would be placed in jeopardy should the Bill not be successful this time – that old familiar threat: shall the country 'now pause in the career of improvement, while . . . other nations adopt the means of aggrandisement which we reject.'

Inevitably, the opposition thundered again. But now there was less to cling to, and no gleeful days duplicating the embarrassment of George Stephenson. The Rennies and Charles Vignoles were impressive witnesses, and the railway committee was helped by positive reports from the Stockton and Darlington line. There were some accidents to trespassers and many delays caused by breakdowns and faults on the track, but predominantly the railway was a great success. At one annual meeting, its shareholders were told how satisfied they must be to find that their opinions, which 'were by many considered empty and delusive, proved to have had their foundation in clear and enlightened views of the best means of promoting the interests of commerce, and diffusing general prosperity.' Within a year of its opening, the price of coal at Stockton had fallen from 18 shillings per ton to 8 shillings and sixpence.

A railway share from 1826, bringing Liverpool and Manchester closer than ever.

THE MEMBER FOR LIVERPOOL believed it his duty to support both the canal owners and the railway promoters, but saw that a new line would eradicate the canal's monopoly, improve competition and efficiency and perhaps in time benefit both forms of transport. In the years since the railway was first proposed, Huskisson had received a steady stream of correspondence both for and against. At the Board of Trade, this correspondence increased in both frequency and pitch. In October 1824 John Gladstone, the Liverpool merchant MP, wrote to Huskisson of the great stock of goods that patiently wait in Liverpool before they can be transferred to Manchester, and of the absurd fee charged by the canals for their eventual journey. He noted that the shares in the Mersey and Irwell canal, commonly known as the Old Navigation, had risen from their issue price of £70 to £1,250, but only the directors benefited at the expense of the merchants, bankers and other locals. 'Surely it is the bounden duty of the Government to support [and] of the Legislature to protect, every fair and honest application that will afford the means of relief.'

As a minister in the mid-1820s, Huskisson felt unable to sit on the Commons committees which discussed the private railway bills, but he supported it plainly in the main debates of the House. He was a shareholder in canals in other counties, and he appreciated their limitations. 'Additional accommodation is wanted for the . . . traffic,' he wrote to one Liverpool correspondent. 'I feel it incumbent upon me to support any plan brought forward by my Constituents for conferring these advantages upon their Trade.'

Huskisson had addressed the matter as the first bill was passing through the Commons in March 1825, again upsetting the ultra Tories in his support of improvement. He claimed it was his duty to back the railroad irrespective of his personal interest, and would have done so had he still been the Member for Chichester. He was encouraged by a recent announcement that the directors of the proposed railway would hold no more than ten shares each in the venture, perceiving that

> it was the great interest of the trading community, and not the profits that might be derived from the shares, which had mainly actuated those individuals to call for the railway.

To Huskisson, the subscribers to the Liverpool and Manchester Railway 'had a higher object in view'. He revealed that he had previously met the directors and insisted that they limit their profits to ensure his support. They told him they would be happy with a profit of 10 or even 5 per cent. He was doubtful whether the canal owners' assertion that there were already sufficient means of transport in the area were correct; he noted that recently cotton had been detained at Liverpool for a fortnight; that manufacturing labours at Manchester had been reduced for as long; and that goods produced in Manchester for foreign parts were not transmitted from the Mersey ports until much delay, a situation that in time would lead to cancelled orders. 'The railway company said they would transmit goods, not only at less charge, but with greater facility than the canal companies could do,' Huskisson said.

> These were the great points to be looked to. We, who maintained a commercial rivalship with all the countries in the world, ought to look to dispatch – ought to look to economy – for the purpose of securing our present advantages.

The chief object of the railway project was just this: to confer benefit on the commerce of the country.

'It was said that there were two or three canals which were sufficient for every purpose of commerce in the districts through which this railway was to pass,' Huskisson explained. 'That assertion, however, was not sufficient to stop the progress of this work.'

The Liverpool MP then quoted some figures regarding the vast increase in the amount of goods exported from the docks in just three years – from £11.5 million in 1821 to £19 million in 1824 – much of which had been transported to the town by the overladen canals. Clearly, this increase would not soon reverse itself. 'Under these circumstances . . . the projected railway ought to be carried into effect.'

With the second attempt, the railway directors again implored him to help with its passage. 'Without it I feel confident that it will be lost,' John Moss wrote to Huskisson.

What chance can we, a few Liverpool merchants, have against Lord Derby . . . who asks for votes as a personal favour to himself? Much of our success in the Commons is ascribed to you, and we must throw ourselves upon your kindness for a little help in the Lords.

Huskisson turned to the Tory manager William Holmes to work a trick or two, and Holmes responded positively. 'Your Liverpool friends need not be alarmed,' he told Huskisson at the beginning of April 1826 when the final bill passed to the House of Lords. 'For I pledge myself that they shall have 18 to 25 peers in the Committee, and I really do not believe that there will be found 5 Peers to vote against them. I do not know what the Devil it is that alarms them.'

Principal opposition in the Lords came from the Earl of Derby and the Earl of Wilton, but the Bill passed on the third reading without amendment, and on 5 May it received royal assent. Henry Booth celebrated with brisk claims upon posterity. 'The contest is over, and the result will be satisfactory to all who contemplate with pleasure the commercial prosperity of the country,' he said,

or who take an interest in marking those great steps in the progress of mechanical science [which has] contributed in no small degree to raise this country to its present preeminence in wealth, power and civilization.

But the two-year process had been damaging to the proprietors' pockets. The passage of the bills through both houses had cost them in excess of £70,000, and the sum led to calls for reform. It was the attitude that was wrong, suggested the *Monthly Review* in London. 'The moment a scheme that is likely to be beneficial to the country is proposed,' it claimed, 'it is treated as a public nuisance by the parliament . . . as a general offence against the nation, which is only to be expiated by a huge tax.'

The money was one thing, but there was a deeper malaise. The troubling and elongated process which the railway directors endured, had, the *Monthly Review* believed,

a direct tendency to deaden energy, to oppress the spirit of enterprise, and make ingenious and able men feel that they would do infinitely better by following the jog trot life of common-place beings . . .

Sandars, Lawrence and Booth were anything but common-place. The minutes from their meetings display an adventurous and ruthless streak: to begin with, they resolved to withhold fees from their fellow directors if they turned up more than five minutes late. The meetings occurred every Monday at noon, except on 12 June 1826, which was transferred to the Friday to accommodate the successful return of William Huskisson in the general election.

Within days of their victory in Parliament, the railway directors had recalled George Stephenson and set up an ugly battle with Charles Vignoles. Parliament had already witnessed the difference in the two men's temperaments, and now it was the turn of the men to face each other. Stephenson resolved to get the details right this time, and seemed to have little time for petty revenge. His principal intention was straightforward: he was finally free to build the greatest railway the world had ever seen.

BY THE BEGINNING of the nineteenth century, the coal mines of Scotland and the north-east of England had experienced a transformation that improved their fortunes and would soon improve all industry: the rails that moved coal from the face to the shafts, and from the pit heads to the canals, were no longer constructed from wood but from cast iron. It was a dual development: some wooden rails were overlaid with a thin strip of iron to extend their life, and other lines, made entirely from flat iron 'plate rails', were laid on wooden sleepers with two-inch lips (or 'flanges') to keep the wheels on course. As with the earlier wagon ways, almost all the trucks were propelled by a combination of gravity and horses.

After 250 years of only moderate improvements in railway track, a great force took hold. The developments prompted by the expansion in small private routes formed the basis for the world's first public railway boom; the arteries of Empire and the New World had their heartland in the furnaces of Nanpanton in Leicestershire and Bedlington in Northumberland.

The first solid iron rails were cast by William Jessop for a private track between a canal dock at Loughborough and Nanpanton in 1789. These 'edge-rails' – so called because they were not solid but formed a T-shape by being wide at the top and narrow through their middle – were first made in 3-foot strips and needed far less daily maintenance than the plate-rails which required constant cleaning to rid them of the dirt and stones that gathered in their right-angles. But they proved extremely brittle. Jessop strengthened the regular rail by giving the central supporting section a curved or 'fish-bellied' structure, but the biggest single improvement came between 1808 and 1820 with the introduction of wrought or malleable iron rails, a rail that emerged from rolling, stretching and beating rather than from being cast in a mould. The rails were broader than the cast-iron strips, contained fewer impurities and could be made to far greater lengths.

George Stephenson decreed that for the Liverpool and Manchester Railway only wrought-iron fish-bellied edge-rails should be used, despite the fact that he and William Losh had formerly taken out a patent for improved cast iron manufacture. They would be supported by cast-iron 'chairs' three feet apart, and these would be placed on 177,000 sleepers, 127,000 to be made from stone and 50,000 from large blocks of Scottish oak, the latter providing more secure support on less stable surfaces such as moss. The rails weighed 35 lbs a yard, and some 44,000 were required in all, not including replacements for breakages.

Tenders were invited to fulfill this huge order, and it was a stipulation that rigorous weight testing be carried out on the rails before mass production; at the start of 1829, it was still not clear whether locomotives would be used for the entire length of the journey, but it was certain from the traffic on the Stockton and Darlington line that the weight of the engines, and their ability to pull greater weights behind them, was increasing with each technological development. Six companies applied for the production contracts, including a bid from the Butterley Company, the firm established by Benjamin Outram and William Jessop after they had proposed their original Liverpool – Manchester Railway thirty years before. Butterley produced everything from tea urns to the ironwork for Vauxhall Bridge, and was a leading manufacturer of edge-rails from the beginning of the century, but they failed to win the biggest prize. George Stephenson placed his initial orders with John Bradley & Co.of Stourbridge and his old friend Michael Longridge of the Bedlington Iron Company. It was a feature of this railway from the very beginning that friends received special favours.

The Bedlington works employed John Birkinshaw's and John Buddle's patented method of pulling the iron through the rolling mill six times, with its final passage purposely distorted to produce the curvature on its underside. Birkinshaw's 'wedge-form' was an important advance over the brittle solid cast-iron bars, enabling an improvement in strength while reducing weight and cost. Birkinshaw's patent of 1820 reveals some additional ambitions:

The respective rails may be made of considerable length (18 feet I should recommend), by which the inconvenience of numerous joints is reduced, and consequently the shocks or jolts to which the carriages are subject (very much to the injury of the machinery) are also diminished. And in order still further to remedy the evil arising from the joint of the Rail-Road, I propose to weld the ends of the bars together as they are laid down, so as to form a considerable length of Iron Rail in one piece.

Nine years later, Stephenson settled on 15-foot rails and a linkage method that entailed hammering a steel key into their ends. The iron chairs were affixed to the sleepers by a combination of oak plugs, iron spikes and portions of felt soaked in pitch to compensate for inexact fittings. Wooden and steel keys were used to attach the rails to the chairs.

Where the rails rested on sleepers they were two inches deep, and between them their width reached three inches. The ballast – the broken rocks and sand that filled the space around the sleepers – was mainly drawn from the railway's excavation and measured up to two feet deep, with a maximum of one foot below the sleepers, and one foot covering and surrounding them. Along most of the route the chairs and sleepers were entirely concealed, with little more than one inch of rail visible.

Thirty-five miles of track were eventually laid, enough to accommodate sidings to depots and planned links to other routes. The total cost, including chairs, spikes and keys, would amount to £67,912, compared to the £10,991 to be spent on the locomotives and carriages. But the cost of the rails would be open-ended. When he placed his first orders for Birkinshaw's and Bradley's rails, Stephenson hoped they would last about thirty years each, but he was optimistic. Some broke after two and very few lasted more than ten without showing cracks.

As soon as the rails began to arrive, Stephenson was faced with the question of how far apart to place them. In truth he had faced this question several times before, and his calculation was the same as when he constructed his first line at Hetton Colliery in 1822: 4 feet 8 inches. He delayed little over this decision, for it was dictated by the distance between the axles on the existing wooden colliery trucks, a measurement that had evolved over centuries to a point where they now represented the most efficient and secure width for haulage by horse. Now, these very trucks were used to transport his railway-building materials along a temporary track parallel to his permanent Liverpool and Manchester line. Some tracks, such as Jessop's Loughborough and Nanpanton route, had been constructed haphazardly with an extra half-inch to the gauge, and the distance from rail to rail on Stephenson's tracks also gradually increased to 4ft 8 1/2 inches as he requested that the edge of the rails be made smoother and slightly curved to accommodate the flanges of the new locomotive wheels without undue friction where the lip met the track. With this, Stephenson had configured the gauge that remains the standard throughout the industrialised world.

There was one more important decision to be made – the distance between the two sets of parallel tracks – and Stephenson had never faced this one before. The Liverpool and Manchester Railway was the first to be designed with the potential for steam traffic in both directions, and as with so much else on this great experiment no one had yet determined an ideal distance between the two separate lines. For a while there was even debate as to whether four sets of track should be laid, two each for passenger and goods services. One matter was clear: the narrower the gap, the less land would have to be excavated and elevated, and the cheaper the railway would be to build. Stephenson determined that the distance between the lines should be 4ft 4 1/2 inches, until it was suggested that it should be four inches wider, exactly the same as the two tracks to enable exceptionally wide loads to travel through the middle of the railway on the central rails (leaving one on each side). But this narrow distance was decided long before the passenger carriages were built and carriage doors designed, and it was a distance which allowed no room for human misjudgement.

F OR A FEW MONTHS in the spring of 1827, William Huskisson's political career took flight once more. Support for his financial and commercial reforms had diminished since the bank failures at the end of 1825, and his efforts had been focused on a new corn bill and Catholic emancipation. For a brief period at least, he received unbridled support from a new party leader.

George Canning had become Prime Minister in April, after Lord Liverpool was found paralysed with a stroke in his breakfast room (he lived on for a year). The King chose Canning almost by default: his main alternative, the ultra Tory Lord Wellington, had just taken over from the Duke of York as military Commander-in-Chief, while Peel was considered young and inexperienced. Huskisson, still in the shadow of his great friend, was not considered.

Canning's appointment was popular with the people but a disaster for the Ultras. Wellington and Peel both refused to serve under him, and he was forced to recruit from amongst the Whigs. Huskisson retained his position at the Board of Trade and was optimistic of pushing through his novel Corn Law Bill; this did not advocate total repeal but the introduction of a new sliding scale, whereby corn could enter the country but the duty paid would vary according to domestic prices. This passed the Commons but fell at the Lords, primarily due to opposition from the Duke of Wellington.

Huskisson was soon to suffer a fate far greater than the failure of any one political ideal. George Canning died suddenly in August 1827, and Huskisson struggled to recover from this blow for the rest of his life. He lost a great friend and his closest political ally, and he was forced to remodel his career. Huskisson was now forced to lead a faction that he had previously been content to goad and steer from the wings. The Canningites became the Huskissonites, a handful of men with potential influence beyond their number and a desire to shape public policy far beyond the limits acceptable to their colleagues.

In the space of a year, Britain experienced the uncertain talents of four different prime ministers, and under each the popular pressure for reform was resisted in the interests of maintaining stability. These governments ruled with fear in their hearts. Huskisson was judged too radical a man for the times, and by the end of the year he was isolated once more. But he would not go without making a catastrophic error of judgement, or without creating the maximum noise.

Huskisson received the news of Canning's death in the Austrian Tyrol, where he was recuperating from a vague illness and his exertions over the Corn Law. He accepted two jobs from the new Prime Minister Lord Goderich, the colonial office and the Leader of the House, but this new administration soon fell apart amid recriminations about policy direction and the filling of other cabinet posts. Goderich was himself in poor health, and was unable to control the forthright team he had inherited. 'Never surely was there a man at the head of affairs so weak, undecided and utterly helpless,' Huskisson wrote to Lord Granville. The administration ended with a bitter dispute between Huskisson and John Charles Herries, the Chancellor of the Exchequer, over each other's competence and the appointment of the chair of the finance committee. Huskisson threatened to resign, but Goderich beat him to it.

Goderich was replaced at the beginning of 1828 by Lord Wellington, whose military bearing failed to bring the Tories much stability after a year of crisis. Huskisson regarded the Duke as an unfeeling and vain man, and in private correspondence took to calling him Sir Gorgeous. (After Waterloo, Wellington became a celebrity of such magnitude that people would scramble on the floor after a haircut to collect his locks. Or, in a manner befitting one who thought unswervingly highly of his own standing, he would collect them himself, and pass them to an agent to sell them on.)

'The Duke was not a good prime minister,' Asa Briggs has written, 'for he could never understand that political colleagues were not military subordinates, and that policy was a matter of opinion as well as authority.' But he did realise that it would be impossible for him to compose a government of ultra Tories alone, so he resolved to imbue it with a Liberal tone. Huskisson kept his post as Colonial Secretary, affording a seat in Cabinet if not at the centre of domestic affairs (he accepted on the condition that his adversary Herries lose his job), his friend Palmerston became Secretary for War, and the Canningite Charles Grant became President of the Board of Trade.

It was a compromise that met much opposition from Wellington's friends. Harriet Arbuthnot, wife of the Tory politician Charles Arbuthnot, noted in her private journal how she 'would have seen them hanged before I would have taken one of them'. She believed that Huskisson came in on Peel's recommendation and against Wellington's wishes: 'He insists upon Mr Huskisson and will not take office without him. I must say I think Mr Peel very wrong!'

Mrs Arbuthnot enjoyed a close, but not uncritical relationship with Wellington for many years, often enjoying long walks with him during which he would talk openly about his political problems. She has often been described as his mistress (including privately by Robert Peel), though a reading of her diary suggests otherwise. Less ambiguous was her loathing of Canning and Huskisson. She was a great friend of Castlereagh, and her personal distrust of Canning ('a low, deceitful man') was already well fermented before their duel; her dislike of Huskisson was less personal, but she still delighted in the diminution of his influence: 'Mr Huskisson's power is completely destroyed!' she exclaimed after one conflict with the Duke.

Her feelings were also inspired by the frustrations of her husband, who felt he deserved better than to be placed at Huskisson's old post at the Commission for Woods and Forests. 'Mr A relented and agreed to accept the office,' she wrote. 'It has, however, put him very much out of humour, as he thinks it ill treatment after his long services and when such rif raf are in the Cabinet . . .'

In May 1828 Mrs Arbuthnot wrote of a meeting with the financier Nathan Rothschild, in which he detected an elaborate scheme of Huskisson's to take the Duke's place.

He abused Mr Huskisson without measure, said he was a designing, cunning rascal whose object was to upset the Duke's government, and that he had heard that his project was to get the finance committee to recommend a payment to the Bank of £5m this year and that, if this project was carried into execution, we should have another panic like 1825, and that Mr Huskisson would lay all the blame on the Duke, and try to destroy him and raise himself upon the ruins of the country.

This is a wildly imaginative scenario, and Huskisson was more damaged by criticism closer to home. Canning's widow led the charge that Huskisson was sacrificing her late husband's principles for want of office; Wellington was a leader so opposed to Canningite policies that they were bound to fail. Huskisson defended his allegiance at the hustings in Liverpool in the spring of 1828, and rumours spread that he had demanded exacting reassurances on reform from Wellington. Earl Grey wrote to Thomas Creevey how 'Huskisson's friends boast everywhere that corn laws, free trade, Portugal . . . in short everything – have been conceded to him as the price of his accession to the government.' But Huskisson had always been a man of compromise, a realistic reformer rather than a doctrinaire one. As a statesman, he often argued from a humane position of pragmatism rather than from a point of party principle. Above all he was a man of conscience, and on 19 May 1828 his conscience undid him.

Predictably, Wellington's government was hampered by factionalism from the start. The Liberal group was opposed by the Prime Minister and Robert Peel, his Leader of the House, at every turn. Lord Ellenborough, another member of the new government, wrote in his diary that in the first cabinet meeting 'the courtesy was that of men who have just fought a duel.' Wellington's relationship with Huskisson had been lukewarm for years, but now their mutual unease had turned to nervous distrust. The majority of Huskisson's liberal reforms at the Board of Trade had been opposed by the Duke, and he detested his assault on economic nationalism. In addition, he had been suspicious of his alliance with Canning and of their wider political ambitions. Even with Canning dead, Wellington regarded Huskisson as a threat. Some of the Prime Minister's friends expressed their bewilderment as to why he kept Huskisson in office. 'He is a good bridge for rats to run over,' Wellington explained.

Initially, Huskisson's influence appeared to be strong. The Commons agreed to a moderate Corn Law amendment, but it retained more protectionist measures than Huskisson wished. Other issues remained unresolved, including the long-running question of parliamentary reform. Popular pressure for widening political representation had been gathering momentum throughout the decade: the more moderate Tories privately acknowledged that the huge industrial expansions of Manchester, Birmingham and Leeds could not remain unrepresented in London for long. But where would it end?

In May 1828, Wellington's government perceived a way of fortifying the dam. The boroughs of Penryn in Cornwall and East Retford in Nottinghamshire were notoriously corrupt, and Huskisson and his colleagues proposed that their seats be transferred to Manchester and Birmingham. The Ultras feared any increase in industrial representation, preferring instead that the seats be transferred to the neighbouring hundreds where the landed classes still dominated. A compromise was suggested and approved by both Wellington and Huskisson: the Penryn franchise was to transfer to Manchester while the East Retford seat was to be absorbed locally. But the Lords rejected this, refusing to accept the political hotbed of Manchester into the Commons. Huskisson then did something unusual. He acted impetuously.

'For a cool and sensible man his conduct is most extraordinary,' Lord Greville wrote in his diary. 'For he acted with the precipitation of a schoolboy and showed a complete want of all those qualities of prudence and calm deliberation for which he has the greatest credit.'

Huskisson believed he had been betrayed; a compromise was reached to his satisfaction, but when this was overturned by the Lords he was left with nothing. Accordingly, when the East Retford bill came before the House, he voted against his government. He left the House of Commons in a state of distress, and at two in the morning composed a brief letter to Wellington.

I owe it to you, as the head of the administration, and to Mr Peel as leader of the House of Commons, to lose no time in affording you an opportunity of placing my office in other hands, as the only means in my power of preventing the injury to the King's service which may ensue from the appearance of disunity in his majesty's councils ...

To anyone reading this, only one interpretation seemed possible: Huskisson was offering his resignation. Certainly Wellington regarded it as such, and he wasted no time in seeing George IV to discuss a replacement. Huskisson received the following reply a few hours later: 'My dear Huskisson, Your letter . . . has surprised me much and has given me great concern. I have considered it my duty to lay it before the King.'

Huskisson's letter had also given the Duke great pleasure, a perfect method (he believed) of ridding his government of its prickliest thorn; best of all, Wellington would appear to have acted according to Huskisson's wishes, pre-empting any accusations that he had behaved dishonourably out of self-interest.

Huskisson, however, received the Duke's reply with horror. He had not intended to resign, merely to be talked out of it. He was talking to Lord Dudley when Wellington's reply arrived, and Dudley said he would attempt to clear up any confusion immediately. But he returned grim-faced, claiming that Wellington maintained, 'It is no mistake, it can be no mistake, and it shall be no mistake.'

Huskisson then asked Lord Palmerston to make further protests to Wellington, instructing him to inform the Duke that he was quite willing to explain his actions of the previous evening, and expressing surprise that no such explanation had yet been called for. But Palmerston also returned with bad news. Huskisson then tried again himself, and wrote another letter. He claimed that the intention of his original note was 'not to express any intentions of my own, but to relieve you of any delicacy which you might feel towards me . . .' The Duke's answer was unequivocal:

I certainly did not understand your letter of two this morning as offering me any option; nor do I understand the one of this evening as leaving me any. I am convinced that, in these times, any loss is better than that of character.

The Duke wrote this letter in the presence of Harriet Arbuthnot, who was unequivocal in her support. 'I do hope and trust they will all go,' she wrote in her journal of Huskisson's political friends.

We shall never have any peace while they remain . . . The Duke will do nothing unfair, but he says . . . that the only option he had was to accept the resignation or beg him to stay, and the latter he positively would not do, for if he did he ceased to be Minister.

Huskisson made one last attempt to rescue his career, sending yet another letter pleading that his intentions had been misunderstood: he had not intended to be taken at his word, merely to relieve the Prime Minister of 'any personal embarrassment'. But Wellington would hear no more from him. Huskisson then asked the Duke for a meeting with the King, a request Wellington declined to forward until the matter was closed; it is believed that Wellington filled up George IV's diary with other appointments to make a meeting with Huskisson impossible. Huskisson finally accepted his fate a day later, and went abroad to recuperate. His departure was followed within hours by that of Palmerston, Lord Dudley and Charles Grant, relieving the government of all that remained of Canning's party.

The controversy remained the great topic of public gossip for a month. 'Nobody judges fairly,' Charles Greville surmised in his diary.

Motives are attributed to both parties which had no existence, and the truth is hardly ever told at first, though it generally oozes out by degrees . . . Upon receiving Huskisson's letter [the Duke] went to Lord Bathurst and consulted him, and Lord Bathurst advised him to take him at his word . . . I believe that Huskisson had no intention of embarrassing the Duke and none of resigning; but though this breach might have been avoided, from the sentiments which have been expressed by both parties it is evident other differences would have arisen which must have dissolved the Government before long.

That the Duke 'treated Huskisson with some degree of harshness there is no doubt,' Greville concluded. 'On both sides there was a mixture of obstinacy and angry feeling, and a disposition to treat the question rather as a personal matter than one in which the public interests were deeply concerned.'

When the King finally saw Huskisson it was said he was extremely gracious, and expressed the utmost regret at losing him. That was Huskisson's version, at least. Others maintained that the King was glad to have got rid of him and his party. There is no doubt that Wellington's actions were received with extravagant and unconcealed joy by the high Tories. When he attended a dinner some days later he sat in the proudest of glows as Lord Eldon congratulated him and offered 'one cheer more' for the old conservative standards and Protestant ascendancy. Huskisson's actions were denounced particularly harshly by the Whigs, whom one may have assumed would have benefited from the controversy. 'Well, have you read Huskisson's charming compositions of letters that he read [in Par liament] as his own defence?' the irascible Whig MP Thomas Creevey wrote to his stepdaughter Elizabeth Ord. 'Never was there anything so low and contemptible throughout, either in intellectual confusion or mental dirt. In short, thank God he has gone to the devil and can never show again.'

Huskisson and his colleagues would not make amends. Huskisson remained in Parliament, but he was once again in smoldering opposition to his own majority party. He did not emerge from what immediately became known as the East Retford Question with much credit, although his actions – a knack for woeful misjudgement at a time of emergency – provided a fateful portent. The orthodox journal *The Annual Register* described him at year end as a broken man. 'He was directly accused of having sacrificed principle to love of place,' it noted when he joined the Wellington ministry, and sympathies had ebbed from him since this moment.

On the present occasion he appeared to feel that part, at least, of the public confidence was gone; that his late friends considered him as having betrayed them; that his new colleagues scarcely trusted him, though they found him useful . . .

The journal noted that Huskisson seemed anxious to redeem himself by an act that would suggest independence, 'yet he took his opportunity so unfortunately, and followed it up with such a miserable want of steadiness and self-respect, that it left him almost without a public character.' His departure was 'scarcely followed by a single regret'.

Matters were not quite as dark as this correspondent suggested. He still had many friends, and he quickly forgave his opponents. Mrs Arbuthnot noted that Huskisson had made overtures towards Wellington within a week of leaving the Cabinet. He had told a colleague that even though

he never could be in office with him again, yet he should like to see the Duke and express his feeling of regard etc. The Duke, however, appears to resent Mr Huskisson's [final explanatory] speech very strongly and very justly, and will not, I think, be induced to see him, at least not at present.

Despite this rebuff, Huskisson remained widely popular amongst his constituents. He travelled to Liverpool from his home in Eartham whenever his health would allow. And as the decade drew to a close, he found that the town was a place of compelling activity.

'YORE MOTHER is getting her tea beside me while I am riting this and in good spirits,' George Stephenson wrote to his son Robert in South America as the railway line took shape. 'We are getting rapidly on with the tunnal under Liverpool it is 22 feet width & 16 feet high we have 6 shafts and . . . we have also got a great deal done on Chat Moss . . .'

Stephenson's relaxed tone belies the great difficulties he overcame to plan his cuttings and surmount the natural obstacles of hill, rock and quagmire. At the Liverpool tunnel nearly 300 men dug their shafts with pickaxes and shovels, working by candlelight with no ventilation and frequent flooding; there were remarkably few fatalities from this endeavour. The six shafts or 'eyes' were sunk to an equal depth and then joined up by excavating (often with explosives) a tunnel to the left and right, a process which produced a genuine sense of progress. The same could not be said for Stephenson's initial efforts at Chat Moss. 'After working for weeks and weeks, in filling in materials to form the road, there did not appear to be the least sign of our being able to raise the solid embankment a single inch,' he revealed in a speech a decade later.

Chat Moss, which had formerly swallowed men whole.

'Even my assistants began to feel uneasy and to doubt the success of the scheme.' The directors also became alarmed, and considered the costly possibility of a new route. The first signs of hope came after four months. Two hundred men dug four parallel drains across almost four miles, each 48 feet apart. These were then drained and filled with the hardened, dried moss that had been removed. Heather and brushwood were then piled on top, followed by a topping of earth, sand and cinders.

There were financial problems as well, the engineers and their workmen often having to stop work until new money could be found from subscribers or new grants were agreed by Parliament. Despite these difficulties, Stephenson's letter to his son, written just two years after the submission of his first survey to Parliament, contained such faith in the progress of the line that he urged his son to return speedily to England: 'You may depend upon it that if you do not get home soon every thing will be at perfection and then there will be nothing for you to do or invent.' But there were still doubts about how the railway would operate. Stephenson was doubtful whether locomotives would manage the whole journey without assistance. He planned one fixed steam engine at Rainhill,

and a nother at near parr moss also one at the top of the tunnal I want these engines to be contantly moveing with an endless Rope so that the locomotive engines can take hold of the Rope and go on without stopping.

A year later, Stephenson had already begun to reconsider this suggestion. Partly this was due to the return, in November 1827, of his son, whose ambitions had not diminished. On his journey home from Colombia, Robert Stephenson had met Richard Trevithick, who was also returning from abroad; Trevithick was penniless, but cheered a little by the knowledge that his early promotion of the travelling steam engine was no longer being dismissed as a fairground novelty. He was grateful, too, for the £50 Stephenson gave him to complete his journey home.

One of Robert Stephenson's first written observations on arriving at the Forth Street works was one of wonder and concern at the rate of progress: 'So many minds are employed in studying railroads, [that] unless I keep stepping forward someone will step past me.' His main task was to show that the entire journey from Liverpool to Manchester could be accomplished by locomotives alone. Convincing others of this would take the form of a public experiment.

IN THE SPRING OF 1829, a notice appeared in Liverpool's newspapers regarding a trial of locomotive engines to be held in October. A prize of £500 was offered for a machine that best fulfilled a complex list of stipulations: the engine should 'effectively consume its own smoke', it should have two safety valves, it should be supported on springs and not exceed fifteen feet in height or six tons in weight, the wheels should accommodate the (already standardised) distance between the rails of four feet eight inches and a half, and it should be capable of pulling a train of carriages weighing 20 tons, day after day at a speed of 10 miles an hour. The venue of the trials was not specified, but the level track at Rainhill was soon considered the only option; to date, only fourteen miles of the railway had been built.

There were several reasons for the trial. It was hoped it would attract favourable publicity to the new railway; it would provide a rigorous test of the rails; it would settle that fierce debate at the directors' meetings about whether fixed winding engines would be needed to supplement locomotives (one director in particular, James Cropper, remained convinced that fixed engines alone were the answer, a position that created a fierce rivalry with George Stephenson); and it would enable the directors to learn whether the engines made by their principal engineer were really as good as he claimed. Not long before the trials were announced, Henry Booth had received a large assortment of letters 'from professors of philosophy down to the humblest mechanic', each offering advice as to how best to equip his railway. 'Every element, and almost every substance, were to be brought into requisition,' he wrote.

The friction of carriages was to be reduced so low that a silk thread would draw them; the power to be applied was so vast as to render a cable asunder. Hydrogen gas and high pressure steam, columns of water and columns of mercury, a hundred atmospheres and a perfect vacuum . . . Every scheme . . . was liberally offered to the Company.

The desire for publicity was realized within a few days; the news of the trial notified London journalists that there would soon be something to see, and their writings in turn prompted engineers to book their passage from Europe and the United States. 'What mind is there so comprehensive as to embrace all the important consequences to which [the railway] will lead?' *Mechanics' Magazine* asked. 'We think we shall not go too far in saying, that it will produce an entire change in the face of British society.' It was suggested that the railways would make it seem as if all British industry was scattered along its shores. In addition,

Living in the country will no longer be a term synonymous with every sort of inconvenience, and it will come to be a mere matter of choice, whether a man of business lives close by his counting-house, or thirty miles from it . . . We may say of railways, in general, as a worthy gentleman is said to have observed of the Stockton and Darlington line, and with ten times greater probability of seeing our prophesy realized – 'Let the country but make the rail-roads, and the rail-roads will make the country.'

The choice of trial judges generated further attention. The selection by the railway directors of John Rastrick, the steam engineer from Stourbridge who had promoted the Liverpool and Manchester

117

Railway to the parliamentary enquiry, and John Kennedy, the textile engineer from Manchester who was an old friend of Joseph Sandars and an early director of the railway, provoked little controversy, but the news that they were to be sitting alongside Nicholas Wood, from the Killingworth colliery, caused much excitement. Wood had previously written that the railway engine was a magnificent thing, but it should know its place, and that any talk of it travelling at 12 or 20 miles an hour was impractical and damaging. But as the *Monthly Review* noted with delight, the proprietors of the Liverpool and Manchester Railway had decreed, 'with a refinement of cruelty which has no parallel in the annals of poetical justice,' that Wood should be obliged 'to see with his own eyes an almost living exemplification of that which, with all his experience and intelligence (for he has both) he pronounced to be impossible.'

It is likely that George Stephenson was consulted over the technical stipulations of the Rainhill Trials, not least to ensure that the conditions regarding weight and boiler pressure were feasible. His competitors also remarked that he learnt of the trial at least one week ahead of his rivals, but this missed the point. The booming success of his Forth Street works, particularly after his son returned from South America, ensured that his advantage could be valued in terms not of days but of years.

Robert Stephenson spent 1828 improving the fundamentals of his company's locomotive construction, analysing each aspect of design and casting. He began by improving the boiler efficiency achieved by Timothy Hackworth's Royal George, and he finished the year by modifying the position of cylinders and flues and erecting 'blast-pipes' within locomotive chimneys to improve steaming by sharpening the draft on the fire.

The Stephenson name survives alone from this dramatic period, but the Rocket would not have emerged without the design skills of George Phipps and William Hutchinson, or without an important

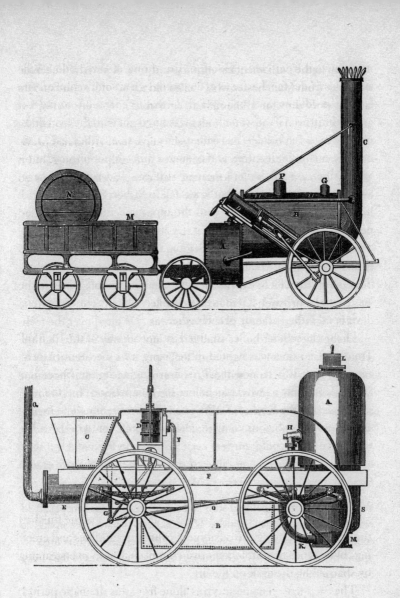

The Rocket and the Novelty in 1829, a diagram from the *Mechanics' Magazine* showing engineers what was possible.

new concept from Henry Booth in the spring of 1829. Booth was able to consider the dynamics of engine design at some remove from factory deadlines, and believed that steam generation would be greatly improved if the water boiler was fitted not with the twin flues present in earlier models but with twenty-five small tubes, each two or three inches in diameter, and of such a thin copper material as to greatly increase the boiler's heating surface. He wrote to George Stephenson with this idea, but it was left to Robert Stephenson and his assistants to experiment with the pipes and fittings and independent firebox that sat behind it. (A similar design for the boiler was drafted in France by Marc Seguin, the engineer on the St Etienne railway, and there followed the inevitable claims on originality. Seguin was the first to the patent office, but Booth and Stephenson were the first to build; it seems entirely likely that the concepts were developed independently of each other.)

The multi-tubular boiler emerged independently of the Rainhill Trials, but no time was wasted in installing it in the Stephensons' entrant. This was named the Premium Engine or the Specimen Engine until only a few weeks before the competition, and the reason it became the Rocket is still open to interpretation. The explanation may be obvious: it was sleek and built for speed, and a suggestive name could impress even before it performed. Or it may have derived from a memorable criticism of the entire steam enterprise in the *Quarterly Review* of March 1825:

What can be more palpably absurd and ridiculous than the prospect held out of locomotives travelling twice as fast as stage-coaches? We should as soon expect the people of Woolwich to suffer themselves to be fired off upon one of Congreve's ricochet rockets as trust themselves to the mercy of such a machine going at such a rate.

(Colonel William Congreve developed his military rocket in 1804, a weapon that could be launched from two miles away and was used to great effect in the American – British naval battles of 1812. The stanza in 'The Star Spangled Banner' – 'And the rocket's red glare, the bombs bursting in air, Gave proof through the night that our flag was still there' – was said to refer to Congreve's missile.)

The official Rainhill papers name the sponsors of the Rocket as George Stephenson and Henry Booth, although it is clear that Robert Stephenson was responsible for its construction. Apart from its novel boiler, the Rocket displayed an innovative alignment of piston and driving wheel, the principal of which could be seen in steam engines a century later. The piston was set at an angle, and provided a direct drive to the wheels rather than the complex 'grasshopper' alignment of overhead beams and joints seen on the likes of Puffing Billy. This was a refinement of the Royal George of 1827, and of the Stephensons' Lancashire Witch of a year later, this last a locomotive that had proved successful hauling coal wagons up modest inclines on the Bolton and Leigh Railway. The Lancashire Witch was also the first to run on steel springs, another vital development that featured on almost all subsequent machines. In this way the Rocket combined new ideas with recent improvements, and is likely to have emerged in this period even without the incentive of a competition. In fact, it was the forty-sixth engine on the Stephensons' order books.

AT THE END OF JULY, as if to whet the public's appetite for the locomotive trial and confirm that it was no idle exercise, an open day was held at the gas-lit tunnel at the mouth of the railway. Admittance was one shilling, for which brave people could accompany the mayor on a stroll through a subterranean vault 70 feet below the pavement. Visitors were not disappointed. 'We cannot well conceive anyone so destitute of curiosity, to use no higher a term, as

Robert Stephenson, who came back to Newcastle just in time.

not to desire to behold a work so unique in its kind,' the *Liverpool Courier* reported. Had anyone suggested five years ago that

in this deep and solemn sanctuary he should meet crowds of well-dressed company and listen to the cheerful sound of many voices, such wild antic- ipations might well have been considered the day dreams of a visionary, or the fanciful wanderings of a too fervent imagination: yet this is but the sober reality.

The Rocket underwent pre-trials before its arrival in Liverpool. At the beginning of September 1829 it spent several days at Nicholas Wood's Killingworth Colliery, pulling wagons loaded with forty men up gentle gradients, and Robert Stephenson seemed delighted with its success. 'On the whole the Engine is capable of doing as much if not more than set forth in the stipulations,' he wrote to Henry Booth. It reached 12 miles an hour, but those who saw it believed it was capable of something much faster. The Rocket arrived in Liverpool at the end of the month.

In a communication issued only days before the trials began, the Rainhill judges defined the particulars of what they called 'the ordeal'. The engines were required to run one-and-three-quarter miles each way, including a quarter of a mile to get up steam at one end and stop at the other. Each engine would make ten trips, a total distance slightly greater than the entire length of the railway. The engine would then go back to the starting post, be brought fresh supplies of fuel and water, and perform ten trips more.

The competition was not a race, and each engine would be given its own day to prove itself. As it turned out, the trial lasted more than a week. On the first day, five entrants were expected – the Rocket, the Sans Pareil designed by Timothy Hackworth, the Novelty designed by John Braithwaite and John Ericsson, the Perseverance designed by Timothy Burstall and the Cycloped of a local barrister named Thomas Brandreth, the latter a bizarre contraption that disregarded almost every rule of the trial and thus instantly won the hearts of all those who saw it.

There was another reason for the Cycloped's appeal: it involved animals. Brandreth was a former director of the Liverpool and Manchester Railway, his departure from the board hastened by his belief that steam locomotives were forever breaking down and blowing up on the Stockton and Darlington line, and should have no place within the current project. Brandreth still favoured horses, a

123

familiar and reassuring fixture of the early colliery lines; their appearance at the Rainhill trial was a reminder of how much the railways had developed in twenty years. Traditionally, horses and donkeys had been employed to pull wagons of coal and iron along upward tracks, and were then untethered for the downhill journey. On some routes animals became passengers, riding at the back of empty open trucks known as dandy cars. Initially horses had to be enticed onto these wagons by filling them with hay, but soon the free ride became an anticipated ritual; when no empty cart was attached for the animals, they would climb onto the backs of full coal trucks rather than endure a walk. But the inventor of the Cycloped found them other uses. Two horses were tied to a moving platform, their trotting motion driving the attached wheels at a steady 5 miles an hour. This abolished the need for safety valves, pressure gauges and angled pistons, and the only steam present emerged from the animals' nostrils; typically, the Cycloped drew loud cheers during its brief appearance, although no one but the horses believed they had a shot at the prize.

One of the stars of The Cycloped, the people's choice.

THE TRIAL BEGAN on 6 October, and attracted thousands of observers. Among the crowd were many engineers from abroad, and it was clear that the Rainhill competition was not just an experiment for a local endeavour. The visitors were made welcome, not least because their hosts realised that if the railway was a success, foreign orders would fill the order books of the Stephensons', Braithwaite and Ericsson and the Bedlington works for years to come. But the impact would be greater still: railways abroad would be made by the same men who had conquered Chat Moss – Irish labourers fleeing famine, heading to the New World from the Liverpool docks.

In fact, the impact of the experiment had already been felt. The first steam locomotive to be tried on an American railroad, on 8 August 1829, was the Stourbridge Lion, designed by the Rainhill judge John Rastrick. Built a year earlier to carry anthracite from the mines at Carbondale to the Delaware and Hudson Canal, its own trial had been made exclusively on British rails by Horatio Allen, who had not long returned from visiting George Stephenson in Liverpool.

From September 1829, the *Niles' Weekly Register* of Baltimore provided regular updates of the construction of the Liverpool and Manchester railway and the locomotive trials, including the advice of one Liverpool resident to the engineers of the Baltimore and Ohio line: 'Be in no hurry in pushing your road, for what is going on here will gain you much information, and save you a great deal of money.' A contributor to the *American Rail-Road Journal* would subsequently remember Rainhill as 'one of the most sublime [feats] of human ingenuity and human daring the world ever beheld.' But London's *Mechanics' Magazine* presented a less than charitable view of the American presence at Rainhill.

It must be confessed . . . that as yet the Americans are considerably behind us in all that relates to railways and steam carriages; and in this, as in other matters, incline but slowly to a reciprocal system. They treasure up all the good things devised on this side of the Atlantic, but favour us with very few of their own in return.

The Liverpool newspapers wrote of other prominent visitors to Rainhill, including their local representative William Huskisson, who was said to be excited by what he saw and eager to have the entire line finished. He hoped the railway would benefit all classes of the local workforce. With regard to the locomotive trial, he did not express a preference for one engine over another.

The MP had ridden on the railway six weeks before, in a carriage pulled by the Twin Sisters, the Stephensons' most efficient engine before the Rocket. Its operation was almost smokeless, a feature remarked upon with pleasure by all who sat behind her. 'Huskisson visited the greater part of the Line with the Directors,' George Stephenson wrote to Michael Longridge at the end of August.

Of course, I was one of the party. We went first to the great Viaduct, then along the line to the skew bridge at Rainhill. Then to the commencement of the deep cutting at Olive Mount where we were met by the Locomotive Engine which took the whole party amounting to about 135 through the deep cutting at the rate of 9 miles an hour to the great delight of the whole party ... The whole went off most pleasantly without the slightest accident attending our various movements. Huskisson expressed himself to me highly delighted with what he had seen ...

The first day of the Rainhill Trials was no more than a warm-up. The Rocket, newly painted in sunflower yellow with a white chimney, ran for a few miles and pulled 13 tons at between 12 and 15 miles an hour. The Cycloped drew fifty people a short distance before the horses demanded a break for hay. A late entry was provided by two men who harnessed themselves to trucks and pulled six passengers at walking speed. But the greatest excitement was caused by the Novelty, which reached almost 30 miles an hour unloaded, an unimaginable speed before the day began.

The Novelty swiftly established itself as the competition favourite. It looked the part, a sleek, light cart with a vertical boiler, mechanical bellows and a single driving cylinder fixed almost vertically above its wheels; it was almost two tons lighter than the Rocket, and appeared to be more like a roadworthy milk truck than anything that had yet appeared on rails. It had been constructed in London in less than two months, where the lack of laid rails meant that it had yet to be fully tested when it arrived at Rainhill. Its designers were an odd pairing: John Ericsson was a young Swedish army captain, while John Braithwaite was an established engineer whose design for the world's first steam fire engine had already proved effective in dealing with blazes at the House of Commons and the Opera House. They were supported by Charles Vignoles, who rode on the engine for the trials and would have liked nothing more than to triumph over George Stephenson. He had resigned from the Liverpool and Manchester project in February 1827 after many disagreements with its chief engineer over survey errors and staff appointments. Vignoles continued to find him boorish and unable to accept criticism, and referred to him always as 'that colliery brakesman'.

The Novelty's biggest triumph came when it pulled a wagon of forty-five people, among them a reporter for the *Mechanics' Magazine*.

We can say for ourselves that we never enjoyed anything in the way of travelling more. We flew along at the rate of a mile-and-a-half in three minutes, and though the velocity was such that we could scarcely distinguish objects as we passed them, the motion was so steady and equable that we could manage not only to read, but write.

The glory was to be short lived, for the second day brought disaster. After one loaded trip at 20 miles an hour in terrible weather, its bellows burst and it was withdrawn for repairs. It would struggle to reach this speed again, and when it did a boiler joint blew out due to soft cement. Its owners withdrew it with heavy hearts.

Timothy Hackworth's Sans Pareil resembled a slimmed-down version of his Royal George, featuring four coupled wheels rather than six, and producing a powerful and consistent steam blast that led the Stephensons and Booth to consider it their greatest competitor. Accordingly, they weren't slow to point out that its weight exceeded the maximum specified in the rules, a feature that was recognised but permitted by the judges. The Sans Pareil soon had other problems. On two separate trial days it developed faults that took hours to repair – a burst pipe and a faulty pump – and it was unable to complete its runs.

Timothy Burstall's Perseverance, an engine that offered little new beyond its impressive central chimney, suffered severe damage when its transporting wagon overturned on its journey from Edinburgh to Liverpool, and its subsequent performance at Rainhill was slow and unwieldy.

The Rocket was run at Rainhill on four separate occasions, but it had won by its second appearance. On Thursday 8 October it covered its first thirty-five miles in three hours and ten minutes, and its next thirty-five in 2 hours and 52 minutes. Its speed with a full train of wagons reached 16 miles an hour over the short tracks, and 30 miles an hour when detached, but it was its reliability that impressed the most; it was a beautifully constructed machine, quite free from the leaks and breakages that hampered its rivals.

Its performance inspired *The Scotsman* to declare that its principles provided 'a greater impulse to civilization than it has ever received from any single cause since the press first opened the gate of knowledge to the human species at large.'

The Rocket's displays on subsequent days only enhanced its reputation, and the judges had no choice but to award it the prize. By the final day it was the only locomotive still moving. The fact that it had been entered by the railway's chief engineer and the company's treasurer was, in the end, quite coincidental.

Two days after the completion of the trial, John Dixon, one of George Stephenson's assistant engineers, wrote to his brother with an account of the competition. He described each engine in turn, comparing the look of the Novelty to 'a new tea urn' and the Sans Pareil to an empty beer barrel rolling around on a pavement. He could be forgiven for favouring the locomotive of his employer, but in doing so he used an unusual phrase: 'Rocket is by far the best engine I have ever seen for Blood and Bone united . . .'

Not long after the trial had concluded, reports of the proceedings began appearing in journals throughout the world. All were full of the joys of steam; often, reporters found it hard to believe what they had just witnessed. In the United States, the *Albany Evening Journal* spoke breathlessly of 'a magnificent prospect . . . an unparalleled opportunity,' while in London the *Quarterly Review* echoed the predictions of Booth and Sandars from years before:

What a cheap and rapid communication could be established, by means of this conveyance, between London and all the great provincial towns! The distance between London and Manchester or Liverpool is two hundred miles, which cannot be travelled at present in a shorter time than twenty hours, and at an expense of at least three pounds.

The journal calculated that a railway would make the journey in ten hours at the cost of between 16 and 18 shillings.

The correspondent, who signed himself ART, was just as impressed with the safety of the operation. 'It is the peculiar excellence of the power of steam that it is at all times under our most perfect command . . .' At the Rainhill Trial

the engines could be stopped, even when going at their utmost speed of thirty miles an hour, by merely reversing the power of the steam. Another advantage is, that those vehicles, from their great weight, and their confinement on the tracks of the railway, can scarcely be overturned by any contingency.

Despite this, the writer considered the ideal speed to be around 20 miles an hour, a rate that would ensure the greatest safety and comfort. Go faster and the journey may become unpleasant. It would be

imprudent . . . to adopt the utmost limit of thirty miles, because such an unusual rate of velocity, surpassing that of the swiftest horse, would be alarming, if it were not dangerous; and if any accident were to happen, such as the vehicle running against any obstacle, a circumstance, no doubt, very unlikely to occur, the effects of the collision would prove fatal both to the vehicle and the passengers.

O N 23 June 1828, not yet a month since Huskisson's political undoing, Harriet Arbuthnot was still revelling in his departure. 'Every thing is again going on quietly,' she wrote in her diary. 'The Huskisson party will soon be quite forgotten or only remembered to be laughed at. There is not one of them that is not dying to be in again . . .' Mrs Arbuthnot did well out of this, as a reshuffle made her husband Charles Chancellor of the Duchy of Lancaster.

Huskisson concerned himself with constituency matters and delivered strong speeches on commerce (promoting familiar reductions in silk and sugar duties), on the economy (the role of the Bank of England) and foreign matters (the relationship with Portugal, Mexico and Africa). 'His manner, when he first entered on his subject, was cold, almost heavy,' the *Spectator* observed.

The secret of his oratory lay in the facility with which he could bring a number of facts to bear upon his argument, and in the soundness and comprehensiveness of his general views. He was not an opponent with whom it was difficult to grapple, for he disdained all slippery arts of avoiding an antagonist; but he was one whom the stoutest champion found it impossible to throw.

His interest in Indian affairs resulted in an offer to become Governor of Madras, but he declined on account of his health. Besides, there were more pressing matters at home. In 1829 Westminster was preoccupied with the Bill for Catholic Emancipation, a reform which enabled Roman Catholics to take a seat in the House of Commons, a measure opposed by the Ultras but wholeheartedly endorsed by Huskisson just as Canning had endorsed it before him. On the other central reform issue he also voted with his party. Despite his position on the East Retford question, and his belief that Manchester should receive representation at Westminster, Huskisson remained firmly against extensive parliamentary reform. His youthful experiences in Paris had warned him against dramatic constitutional change. In Huskisson's mind, there was no telling where it would end: 'Whenever an occasion arose of great popular excitement or reaction, the consequence would be a total subversion of our constitution,' he announced in February 1830, 'followed by a complete confusion and anarchy, terminating first in the tyranny of a fierce democracy and then in that of a military despotism . . .' He resolved to give such a notion his staunchest opposition for as long as he had a seat in Parliament.

THE ROCKET was not a very easy engine to drive, and it was an even harder one to stop. Like all the locomotives of the period, it was prone to minor mishaps – cracks at its joints and pressure points, loss of power due to loose fittings – and accidents would occur at unlikely times. On one test run over Chat Moss, the engine did well – four miles over the marshland with a train of wagons and passengers in seventeen minutes – but on its onward journey to Manchester, where the road was still unfinished, it was thrown off the rails by the breaking of one of its smaller wheels, and with it went the water carriage and some of the wagons. There were forty people on board at the time, at a speed approaching 24 miles an hour, and none of them were injured. The train took more than a hundred yards to stop after the wheel broke, which was considered satisfactory. One of the passengers regarded it as proof 'that travelling rapidly on the railway will be by no means so dangerous as many persons have supposed'.

The man entrusted with control of the Rocket on opening day was Joseph Locke, a twenty-five-year-old assistant engineer at the Stephenson works who had impressed his masters with his ambition and technical dexterity. But Locke's early days had not promised much. He grew up in Barnsley, left school at thirteen, and took a succession of menial jobs with local surveyors. In 1823 he was working as a clerk at his father's colliery when it received a visit from George Stephenson on the search for unpaid staff for his new engine works on Tyneside.

At Forth Street Locke flourished as never before, supplementing his growing knowledge of steam mechanics with evening classes in mathematics and draftsmanship. Stephenson recognised Locke's potential and by 1827 had begun rewarding him with a salary and responsible surveying assignments. He became one of Stephenson's leading assistants on the Liverpool and Manchester line, responsible for the construction of the first ten miles of the railway out of Liverpool, including the Wapping tunnels and the Olive Mount excavation.

But the two men fell out not long before the Rainhill Trials. Locke had become great friends with Robert Stephenson, and the pair had conducted a survey of several collieries and composed a report proposing that locomotives would always be faster and cheaper than the fixed rope haulage engines favoured by several directors of the Liverpool and Manchester Company (one early proposal involved installing fixed engine houses every mile and a half along the route). As chief engineer, George Stephenson insisted that he assumed sole authorship of the report, and a serious quarrel ensued. Robert Stephenson brokered a compromise that included all their names on the final document, and it is believed that it was Robert who insisted that Locke should play a responsible part at the opening ceremony. In fact, George Stephenson had little choice: there were only a handful of men with the expertise to control the sort of machines he had brought forth.

A YEAR BEFORE the railway opening, the water men had still not abandoned opposition or hope. James Loch MP, a personal advisor to the canal owner Lord Stafford, wrote to Huskisson with the prospect of several new canal routes that would yet make the railroad (which he abbreviated to R.R. because he couldn't bear to think of it whole) superfluous. He spoke hopefully of

a scheme to make a new harbour at Dalpool on the Dee and to convert it by a ship canal with a set of new docks at Walazee Pool, opposite Liverpool, with a side canal to Chester and joining the Duke's Canal at Preston Brook . . .

In 1829, Loch gave up some of Christmas Day to compose another lengthy protesting letter, and there was desperation in his tone; he knew that the Liverpool and Manchester Railway would open sometime in the next year unless some fantastic fate befell it. His present campaign was also directed against the other permanent rail schemes that he feared would soon contaminate the entire region. 'The late experiments at Liverpool have given rise to a vast variety of projects,' he wrote,

many of them ill-imagined, all got up in extreme haste – adopted on little rational principle – promoted by scheming attorneys and prepared by young and rash engineers, and entered into by people impatient of low interest for their money . . .

Loch was willing to make concessions. 'In regard to the carriage of light goods and passengers, the probability is that R.R. will have no competitors . . .' But such matters were still to be subject to 'serious investigation, and of doubtful result whether they will carry heavy and bulky goods cheaper than canals.'

Loch had one request – that all current railroad building schemes be subject to a moratorium, a delay that would provide time for the canal owners' interests to be further considered – perhaps there could be compensation – and for the railway investors to reconsider their sudden enthusiasms. Loch had recently been told of a plan whereby the concerns of the canals and railways may unite: it was proposed that a railway branch line be built from the Liverpool and Manchester line to Runcorn Gap and there cross the Mersey, to meet the Duke's Canal or towing path to Preston Brook, and then proceed by a new line to Namptwich, where it would meet the Birmingham and Liverpool junction canal works, and advance by Birmingham to London. Loch wrote that, even though this complex journey might benefit Lord Stafford and other canal owners, it too should be subject to delay and intricate consideration before a rash shovel was pitched.

'I have not conveyed the above proposal to Government without much consideration,' Loch informed Huskisson.

[But] it can never be advantageous to a country that much of its capital should be unnecessarily annihilated and a vast number of persons dependent on the existence of that capital reduced to poverty, except such a sacrifice is demanded on the clearest public necessity, founded on incontrovertible general principles.

And there was one more thing. 'The Mersey and Irwell shares have fallen from £1250, which they were three years ago – to £650.'

134

James Loch's letter was copied to many people, including Henry Booth and John Moss, by then Deputy Chairman of the Liverpool and Manchester Railway. Moss had himself written to Huskisson several times, proffering an alternate view. In his analysis, the iron rail was unstoppable, and would soon reach the capital. 'Provided our Liverpool and Manchester Railroad answers our expectations,' he wrote in December 1829, 'that is, if goods and passengers CAN be carried at less than half the present prices, [then] no one can doubt but a railroad will be made between Liverpool and London.'

Publicly at least, Moss was eager to appease the canal owners and protect their interests as best he could. 'Our work is to injure as little as possible . . . our appointment is one of conciliation . . . I think we can prove to each person whom we call upon that it is for their interest to go with us.'

As he wrote, Moss was already named as the director of two other proposed railways, and four more that planned to join the Liverpool and Manchester line. In a rare shade of doubt, he confessed to Huskisson, 'I am one of those who fear that we shall have more to do than we can do well.'

JOSEPH LOCKE and the other engine directors had been out on the line several times in the high summer of 1830, and George Stephenson had been a tireless instructor as they learnt to cope with their new machines. 'Every engine-man must be provided with all necessary tools and implements for the immediate repair of accidents,' he wrote to the directors. He meant accidents to the engines and the rails. 'He must also be provided with three signal flags, viz. – white, red and purple: the white flag signifying "Go on", the red flag "Go slowly (and) hold down the brake", the purple flag "Stop".'

Excavating Olive Mount: the beginning of the journey.

There was guidance too on how to hold the flags. A flag held aloft was to be observed only by the carriages or engine to which it belonged. A flag held sideways was a signal for the next approaching engine to fall back or advance as required. The trains were ordered to keep 100 yards apart when moving at below 12 miles per hour, and 200 yards apart when moving faster. The overall speed limit was set at 18 miles per hour.

In the eleven months between the success of the Rocket at Rainhill and the opening of the Liverpool and Manchester Railway, several new improvements had been made at the Stephensons' works that were incorporated on subsequent smaller engines such as the Planet. These included further advances to the boiler and general improvements in steaming made possible by an integral fire-box rather than the external example on the Rocket. The Forth Street factory had also begun to consider the possibility of fitting their locomotives with brakes.

One of the railway's many test trips carried Thomas Creevey, one of its loudest opponents in Parliament, who couldn't resist discovering for himself whether all he feared about the enterprise was true. Eighteen years before, Creevey had lost an election in Liverpool against George Canning, and had henceforth done everything in his power to dismiss the prominence of the town and those who benefited from it. One may detect a little disappointment in a letter he wrote after the trip: the experience wasn't the disaster he had hoped for – indeed, the only fault he detected concerned unusual damage to clothing.

'Today we have had a lark of a very high order,' he wrote to his friend Elizabeth Ord.

Lady Wilton sent over yesterday to say that the Loco Motive machine was to be upon the railway at such a place at 12 o'clock . . . I had the satisfaction, for I can't call it pleasure, of taking a trip of five miles in it, which we did in just a quarter of an hour – that is 20 miles an hour.

At some point, the engine got up to 23 miles an hour, and Creevey acknowledged how smooth it felt. 'But the quickest motion is to me frightful; it is really flying, and it is impossible to divest yourself of the notion of instant death to all upon the least accident happening.' It gave him a headache for days, and he was certain that his first experience of the railway would be his last. There wasn't much smoke, he admitted, 'but sparks of fire are abroad in some quantity: one burnt Miss de Ros's cheek, another a hole in Lady Maria's silk pelisse and a third a hole in someone else's gown.'

A similar affliction spoilt the nocturnal travellers behind the Wildfire, an engine modelled on the Planet. They reported not only singed clothes but the experience of riding on a moving volcano, its chimney spitting fireballs into the darkness. But passengers were impressed with one detail in particular – the ability of the engine to stop 'almost instantly', a feature which confirmed its superiority over the Rocket.

On 14 June 1830, twenty men went for another test journey from the Engine House, Liverpool to Oldfield Lane Bridge, Salford, two miles shy of the complete route. The directors travelled in two carriages, one closed with wood and glass, the other open to an overcast sky, and they were carried by the Arrow, an engine built to a modified design of the Rocket. Seven loaded coal wagons were attached behind them, and the journey was completed in two hours and twenty-five minutes. The wagons were unhitched for the return journey, enabling the twenty-nine miles to be covered in one hour and forty-six minutes, including two stoppages for water. The speed of the train exceeded twenty-five miles per hour.

The weather for June had been appalling, with the wind frequently blowing debris along the tracks, and yet the tests had all been completed without serious incident. Henry Booth noted that the whole result was 'highly satisfactory', and the railroad was declared safe and almost ready. At a meeting that evening the directors failed to decide upon an exact date for the opening, but it was agreed that it should be late summer. Later that month, after consultation with the office of the Duke of Wellington, the day for the railway's official opening was set for 15 September.

PART THREE

Before The Sun Revolved

THE DUKE was in a carriage lavish even for royalty. Egerton Smith, the editor of the *Liverpool Courier*, described a costly and splendid form of transport that had never been seen before.

The floor – 32 feet long by 8 feet wide, supported on eight wheels, partly concealed by a basement, ornamented with bold gold mouldings and laurel wreaths, on a ground of crimson cloth; an ornamental gilt balustrade extended round each end of the carriage, and united with one of the pillars which supported the roof. A lofty canopy of crimson cloth, 24 feet in length, rested upon eight carved and gilt pillars, the cornice enriched with gold ornaments and pendant tassels, the cloth fluted to two centres, surmounted by two ducal coronets.

But this was not enough. A vast crimson-covered ottoman ran down the centre of the coach, said to accommodate as many as thirty people. Crimson curtains, held back around the pillars, could tastefully be drawn around the entire length of the carriage to screen passengers from bad weather. The Duke's carriage lay in the middle of two other smaller coaches, only slightly less impressive in comfort and design.

This cortege was the work of James Edmondson, a cabinet maker whose work had won him two seats in the pursuing parade. The carriages behind other engines were not quite so lavish, but were lined and cushioned and still resembled the most luxurious of road coaches. They were also adaptable, carrying between 12 and 24 seated passengers inside. Others, without a covering, could carry 60. They had regal names – Royal William, Queen Adelaide – and one bore the name of a patron who had once sent his men out to harm the railway's engineers: Marquis of Stafford.

William and Emily Huskisson were in the ducal car, but they were not sitting with the Duke. There were four carriages in all: the band wagon, a passenger car containing the Huskissons and about twenty-five other dignitaries, the Duke's car, and another carriage with other guests. Communication was difficult even within the same carriage, and not just on account of noise from the engine and the crowds. There was just too much to see – too much novelty – to utter anything beyond excited instructions to look ahead, look left, look there.

'I don't think I ever saw a more beautiful sight than at the moment when the car attached to the engine shot off on its journey,' wrote Harriet Arbuthnot, who was sitting just behind the Duke. She liked the view upwards, along the sides of rock cut on either side of her, and the sight of the crowd waving their handkerchiefs above her head.

A few weeks before her arrival in Liverpool, Arbuthnot had visited the London theatre with the Duke to see Miss Kemble in *Mrs Beverly*. 'I did not like her so well as in Juliet . . . I was not the least affected. She does not speak naturally nor pronounce well, and one never forgets for a moment that she is acting.'

Fanny Kemble was sitting in one of the pursuing carriages, and kept her dramatics for her prose. 'My spirits rose to the true champagne height, and I never enjoyed anything so much as the first hour of our progress,' she wrote to a friend.

I had been unluckily separated from my mother in the first distribution of places, but by an exchange of seats which she was enabled to make she rejoined me when I was at the height of my ecstasy, which was considerably damped by finding that she was frightened to death, and intent upon nothing but devising means of escaping from a situation which appeared to her to threaten with instant annihilation herself and all her travelling companions . . . I had expected her to be as delighted as myself with our excursion.'

Wellington and the Huskissons were on the southerly track, and had it to themselves. The other seven trains were all on the northerly, following the Ducal engine, the Northumbrian, in an orderly procession. The Northumbrian occasionally slowed down to let a few engines parade past, but it soon caught and overtook them.

The first milepost appeared on the left. On the right stood Spekelands, the seat of former mayor Thomas Earle, and the greatest congregation of spectators, and immediately after it was Wavertree Lane Station and Wavertree Hall, the home of Charles Lawrence, the first chairman of the railway committee, set off handsomely by the Wavertree Hills. The station was the first of seventeen along the line.

Some passengers held the pamphlets written by James Scott Walker and Henry Booth a few weeks earlier. Each contained an appendix of arresting facts – fastest journey time so far (1 hour, 26 minutes, including 7 minutes of stoppages); the total number of bridges and viaducts (63); the cost of each bridge (from £91 for the skew archway at Mill Lane to £45,208 for the grand nine-arch Sankey Viaduct); the total cost of the entire enterprise (in the region of £820,000) – but the greatest sense of awe was to be derived from the account of the colossal human strength and ingenuity required for the railway's construction at Chat Moss. Special praise was heaped on those who skilfully drained, levelled and set rails upon the 30-foot-deep pulpy surface, and there were extensive tributes to the 2,250-yard Wapping goods tunnel of Joseph Locke, a work described by Scott Walker as unimaginable "ere science had armed man with God-like powers'.

Of the Sankey Viaduct, over which today's passengers would be crossing in twenty minutes, Booth noted that it required about 200 thick piles of wood, from 20 to 30 feet in length, to shore up the foundation of each of the ten supporting brick piers:

A sketch of the Duke's carriage, and who sat where, once the property of the chairman Charles Lawrence.

The heavy ram employed to impart the finishing strokes, hoisted up with double purchase and snail's pace to the summit of the Piling Engine, and then falling slowly down like a thunderbolt on the head of the devoted timber, driving it perhaps a single half-inch into the stratum below, is well calculated to put to the test the virtue of patience . . .

The travellers journeyed under several of the handsome bridges, arriving at the Olive Mount excavation. This area, two and a half miles from the start, presented an enormous chasm, referred to in Lacey's Liverpool guidebook as being so deep 'as to destroy all idea of it being the work of man . . . we should attribute the passage to some great convulsion of nature.' The sides were already covered with moss and grass, and sunk as much as seventy feet below the level of the countryside. Three hundred yards further there was a gate where cattle would be admitted to the carriages – startled animals gliding their way through a gouged landscape at fifteen miles an hour to the Manchester markets. Once, this landscape was theirs alone.

Another dip in the track, an incline of about 4 feet to the mile, ensured an increase in speed towards Broad Green Station and Summer Hill, the magisterial estate of Thomas Case. The view from the carriage was now extensive, over an embankment that ranged in height from fifteen to fifty feet, and bounded by a line of trees before Childwall and its ancient church burst into view in the distance on the right, followed by the mills of Roby and Woolton, and the outline of Halton Castle.

On the left, the Huskissons may have observed views of equal magnitude: Knowsley Park and Hall, the seat of the Earl of Derby. The dense woods were broken up by the town of Prescot and then the peculiar red bricks of Roby Hall. The village of Huyton appeared after six miles, chiefly notable in the guide books for the majestic screen within its church. To the right was the country house Red Hazels, currently for sale, surrounded by pleasure grounds.

At the Huyton embankment, six and a half miles from Liverpool, there was the beginning of a small adjacent private railway intended to connect Mr Willis's collieries a few hundred yards away; the chimnies and gear were in plain view. On the left was an engine house built to pull the trains up the inclined plane at Whiston, rising 82 feet in a mile and a half, but for passenger trains it was deemed unnecessary. The Rainhill level appeared just beyond the Whiston collieries. A water supply had been installed shortly after the completion of the trials, but none of the engines yet required a stop.

The Rainhill Bridge, with a beautiful skew arch-span of 54 feet, marked the nine-mile mark. It had not been possible to divert either road or railway to make a rectangular crossing, so the bridge crossed the line at an angle of 34 degrees, with the largest sandstone block weighing two tons. The Liverpool and Manchester turnpike road passed over it, and for this ceremonial day a stream of mail-coaches had gathered to view the new competition. A little further along stood Kendrick's Cross Station, another venue where passengers would join and leave the train as soon as the railway opened for regular traffic the next day. The fare to Manchester had already been painted on boards at the ticket office: 4 shillings in closed carriages, 3 in open.

HUSKISSON passed a line of railway cutting to the left, the first signs of a link to Bourne and Robinson's collieries, and immediately afterwards came Lea Green Gate Station, whereupon the engine built up speed as it descended the Sutton incline. Here the gates that prevented people and cattle crossing the line increased in number, and an iron bridge was planned to carry the proposed branch railway between Runcorn Gap and the coalfields of St Helens. Another railway to the left, the St Helen's Junction Line, was also planned; the lines were spreading through the north of England like cracks on shattered glass.

At Parr Moss, thirteen miles along, the carriages seemed to glide as if on ice, the result of a perfect level formed over this formerly swampy plot – at times twenty feet deep – by filling it with the earth and rocks from the Sutton excavation. The correspondent for *Blackwood's Edinburgh Magazine*, who was leading the secondary procession in the Phoenix, here made a novel observation. Among the 'enthusiastic cheers of wondering multitudes', he noticed

a solitary being pursuing his daily work with as much indifference to what was going on as if he had been Robinson Crusoe on his desert island. He was in a field of oats; and there, with measured step, he slowly and leisurely followed the stroke of his scythe without a moment's pause . . . neither head was raised nor eye turned upward.

Shortly before, the writer had been involved in an accident.

One of our engine wheels, how I know not, contrived to bolt from the course – in plain words it contrived to bolt from the rail, and ploughed along upon the clay, with no other inconvenience than an increase in friction . . . The engine, however, behind us, not being aware of our mishap, came pelting on at a smart pace, without receiving its signal for checking motion in time.

There was a hard jolt at the back of the last carriage, 'sufficiently loud and forcible to give an idea of what would happen if by any strange chance it had charged us with the unrestrained impetuosity of its powers.' It was the railway's first train-on-train collision. But there were no reported injuries, the wheel was remounted and the journey resumed.

The Leigh collieries announced the Sankey embankment and Burton Wood, and beyond this the racehorse stables and track of Mr Clarke, trainer to the Marquis of Westminster. On this day, the horses which usually ran free in enclosed pasture were noted to have stood and stared, or to have turned and galloped to the farthest corner of their field.

No.	NAMES OF BRIDGES, Commencing at the Liverpool end.	No. of Arches.	Skew or Square built.	Railway under or over the common road.	Span of the Arch, in feet, on the skew face.	Whether Ashler, Rubble, or Brick Work.
					Ft. In.	
1	Parks' Bridge	1	Square.	Under.	—	Ashler with brick arch, faced with stone.
2	Old Lane Bridge	1	Square.	Under.	—	Brick-work.
3	Wright's Bridge	1	Square.	Under.	—	Brick-work.
4	Rathbone's Lane Bridge	1	Askew.	Under.	38 0	Ashler with brick arch, faced with stone.
5	Sandown Bridge	1	Square.	Under.	—	Ashler.
6	Mill Lane Archway	1	Askew.	Under.	25 6	Brick-work.
7	Wavertree Nook Bridge	1	Askew.	Under.	38 0	Ashler.
8	Ainsworth's Bridge	1	Square.	Over.	—	Ashler.
9	Case's Bridge, No. 1	1	Square.	Over.	—	Ashler.
10	Ditto, No. 2	1	Square.	Over.	—	Ashler.
11	Childwall Lane Bridge	1	Square.	Over.	—	Brick arch and ashler quoins.
12	Pilch Lane Bridge	1	Square.	Over.	—	Ditto.
13	Jamieson's Bridge	1	Square.	Over.	—	Ditto.
14	Lord Derby's Bridge	1	Square.	Over.	—	Ditto.
15	Baron's Bridge	1	Square.	Over.	—	Ditto.
16	Ball's Bridge	1	Square.	Over.	—	Ditto.
17	Huyton Hey Bridge	1	Square.	Over.	—	Ditto.
18	Seel's Bridge	1	Square.	Over.	—	Rubble, with ashler quoins.
19	Lee's Bridge, No. 2	1	Square.	Over.	—	Brick arch and ashler quoins.
20	Ditto, No. 1	1	Square.	Over.	—	Ditto.
21	Whiston Bridge, No. 1	1	Square.	Under.	—	Ditto.
22	Ditto, No. 2	1	Askew.	Under.	47 0	Ashler with brick arch, faced with stone.
23	Makin's Occupation Bridge	—	Unfshd.	—	—	Timber on stone piers.
24	Cumber Lane Bridge	1	Square.	Under.	—	Ashler.
25	Stone Lane Bridge	1	Square.	Under.	—	Wood with stone piers.
26	Spring Lane Bridge	1	Askew.	Under.	54 0	Ashler with brick arch, faced with stone.
27	Rainhill Bridge	1	Askew.	Over.	14 0	Ashler.
28	Bourne's Tunnel	1	Askew.	Over.	14 0	Ashler and rubble.
29	Marshall's Cross Bridge	1	Square.	Under.	—	Ashler.
30	Sutton Bridge	1	Square.	Under.	—	Ashler.
31	Sankey Viaduct	9	Square.	Over.	—	Brick with stone face, quoins & parapets.
32	Legh's Cattle Archway	1	Square.	Over.	—	Brick-work.
33	Sandy Main's Bridge	1	Askew.	Over.	15 6	Brick-work.
34	Newton Bridge	4	Square.	Over.	—	Brick-work, with stone facing
35	Parkside Bridge	1	Askew.	Over.	32 6	Brick-work.
36	Lockingstump Lane Bridge	1	Square.	Under.	—	Brick-work.
37	Kenyon Tunnel	1	Square.	Under.	—	Brick-work.
38	Hardman's Bridge	1	Square.	Under.	—	Brick-work.
39	Newton's Bridge	1	Square.	Under.	—	Brick-work.
40	Broseley Bridge	1	Square.	Under.	—	Brick-work.
41	Withington's Bridge	1	Square.	Over.	—	Brick-work.
42	Duckinfield's Bridge	1	Square.	Over.	—	Brick-work.
43	Bury Lane Bridge	1	Square.	Over.	—	Brick, with stone quoins.
44	Glazebrook Bridge	1	Square.	Ov.Brook	—	Brick, with stone quoins&stone pillasters.
45	Hodgkinson's Cattle Bridge	1	Square.	Under.	—	Brick.
46	Chat Moss (Frame) Bridge	1	Square.	Over.	—	Brick and timber.
47	Legh's Brick Arch	1	Square.	Over.	—	Brick.
48	Worsley Brook, Great Culvert	1	Square.	Ov.Brook	—	Brick.
49	Trafford's Bridge	1	Square.	Over.	—	Brick.
50	Sandy Lane Bridge	1	Square.	Over.	—	Brick and stone quoins.
51	Winton Skew Bridge	1	Askew.	Over.	31 0	Brick and stone pilasters.
52	Canal (Duke's) Bridge	2	Square.	Over.	—	Dressed ashler.
53	Monks' Hall Bridge	1	Square.	Under.	—	Brick.
54	Eccles Bridge	1	Sq. & Askew	Under.	34 0	Brick and stone quoins.
55	Whitaker's Mill Dam					Brick-work and Masonry
56	Stothard's Occupation Bridge	1	Square.	Under.	—	Brick.
57	Gore Booth's Bridge	1	Square·	Under.	—	Brick.
58	Cross Lane Bridge	1	Askew.	Under.	30 3	Brick and stone quoins to arch.
59	Jones's Bridges—No. 1	1	Askew.	Under.	30 4	Brick.
60	No. 2	1	Askew.	Under.	30 3	Brick.
61	No. 3	1	Askew.	Under.	30 3	Brick and stone quoins.
62	Oldfield Lane Bridge	1	Askew.	Under.	33 0	Brick and stone quoins.
63	Irwell Bridge	2	Askew.	Ov.River	65 0	Ashler.

Sundry Culverts, Foot Bridges, and compensation in lieu of Occupation Bridges ....

Henry Booth's meticulous record of bridge construction.

	Description of String Course and Coping.	Abutments, whether Rock, Masonry, or Brick Work.	Width of way, in feet, between Parapets over Arch.	Width of way, in feet, between Side Walls under Arch.	Height under the centre of the Arch, from Railway or common road, in feet.	Slope of common road over the Railway.	Slope of common road under the Railway.	Number of feet common road is raised.	Number of feet common road is sunk.	COST.
			Ft. In.	Ft. In.	Ft. In.			Ft. In.	Ft. In.	£. s. D.
1	Stone.	Masonry.	28 0	30 0	26 9	Level.	—	—	—	741 5 9
2	Stone.	Brick.	12 0	30 0	18 0	Level.	—	—	Unfshd.	156 10 0
3	Stone.	Brick.	15 0	30 0	18 0	Level.	—	—	—	184 5 6
4	Stone.	Masonry.	23 6	30 0	24 3	Level.	—	—	Unfshd.	973 14 2
5	Stone.	Masonry.	15 8	40 0	40 6	Level.	—	—	—	765 13 1
6	None.	Rock.	60 0	30 0	35 0	Level.	—	—	—	91 3 11
7	Stone.	Rock.	20 0	37 6	18 0	1 in 20	—	3 0	—	274 9 4
8	Stone.	Masonry.	34 6	12 6	13 6	—	Level.	—	—	418 5 10
9	Stone.	Masonry.	34 6	12 0	16 0	—	Level.	—	—	418 0 2
10	Stone.	Masonry.	34 6	12 0	16 0	—	Level.	—	—	493 0 3
11	Stone.	Masonry.	66 6	14 0	16 0	—	Level.	—	—	346 12 1
12	Stone.	Masonry.	34 6	16 0	16 0	—	1 in 30	—	5 6	270 1 0
13	Stone.	Masonry.	34 6	12 0	18 0	—	Level.	—	—	202 7 0
14	Stone.	Masonry.	34 6	12 0	20 0	—	Level.	—	—	241 16 1
15	Stone.	Masonry.	34 6	12 0	16 0	—	Level.	—	—	240 9 11
16	Stone.	Masonry.	34 6	12 0	19 0	—	Level.	—	—	204 5 5
17	Stone.	Masonry.	34 6	12 0	12 4	—	Level.	—	—	302 3 2
18	Stone.	Masonry.	34 6	12 0	14 0	—	1 in 30	—	1 6	215 0 3
19	Stone.	Masonry.	34 6	12 0	14 10	—	Level.	—	—	215 8 10
20	Stone.	Masonry.	34 6	12 0	21 10	—	Level.	—	—	282 0 9
21	Stone.	Masonry.	47 6	22 0	18 0	1 in 13	—	14 0	—	960 5 0
22	Stone.	Masonry.	24 0	30 0	18 0	1 in 20	—	15 0	—	1174 0 1
23	.	.	30 0	—	—	—	—	—	—	74 15 2
24	Stone.	Masonry.	16 0	30 0	18 0	1 in 20	—	12 0	—	536 13 0
25	Stone.	Masonry.	9 0	45 0	18 0	Level.	—	—	—	193 15 3
26	Stone.	Masonry.	16 0	30 0	18 0	1 in 30	—	8 0	—	418 19 8
27	Stone.	Masonry.	30 0	30 0	18 0	1 in 26	—	12 0	—	3735 6 7
28	Stone.	Masonry.	104 0	7 0	7 0	—	—	—	—	165 5 0
29	Stone.	Masonry.	24 0	30 0	18 0	1 in 20	—	5 0	—	864 13 10
30	Stone.	Masonry.	26 6	30 0	23 0	Level.	—	—	—	470 8 9
31	Stone.	Brick-work.	25 0	50 0	60 to Canal	—	—	—	—	45,208 18 6
32	None.	Brick.	None.	12 0	6 0	—	—	—	—	257 18 5
33	Stone.	Brick.	35 0	12 0	15 0	—	—	—	—	429 0 1
34	Stone.	Brick.	25 0	30 0	27 0	—	—	—	—	5340 12 5
35	Stone.	Rock.	20 0	30 0	18 6	1 in 18.	—	6 0	—	316 19 6
36	Stone.	Brick.	20 0	30 0	18 0	Level.	—	—	—	491 14 9
37	Stone.	Brick.	—	30 0	19 0	Level.	—	—	—	1703 19 1
38	Stone.	Brick.	12 0	30 0	20 0	1 in 9	—	3 6	—	434 7 9
39	Stone.	Brick.	12 0	30 0	18 0	1 in 12	—	7 0	—	369 12 2
40	Stone.	Brick.	20 0	30 0	18 0	1 in 18	—	7 0	—	663 4 10
41	Stone.	Brick.	35 0	12 0	14 0	—	Level.	—	—	419 15 4
42	Stone.	Brick.	35 0	12 0	14 0	—	Level.	—	—	323 10 3
43	Stone.	Brick.	35 0	16 0	16 0	—	1 in 20	3 0	—	621 1 7
44	Stone.	Brick.	35 0	30 0	30 ab. Riv.	—	—	—	—	1758 8 6
45	Stone.	Brick.	35 0	9 0	10 0	—	—	—	Unfshd.	13 9 0
46	Stone.	Brick.	25 0	12 0	13 0	—	—	—	—	466 19 6
47	Stone.	Brick.	25 0	16 0	16 0	—	Level.	—	—	513 9 6
48	Stone.	Brick.	125 0	13 0	13 to Wat.	—	—	—	—	1598 5 8
49	Stone.	Brick.	60 0	12 0	13 0	—	—	—	—	689 6 0
50	Stone.	Brick.	25 0	16 0	21 0	—	Level.	—	—	1098 18 4
51	Stone.	Masonry.	25 0	22 0	20 0	—	Level.	—	—	1725 10 5
52	Stone.	Masonry.	25 0	25 0	12 to Wat.	—	Level.	—	—	1158 8 11
53	Stone.	Red Rock.	36 0	30 0	18 0	1 in 18	—	6 0	—	453 19 11
54	Stone.	Red Rock.	48 0	30 0	18 0	1 in 24	—	6 0	—	954 0 1
55	....									631 10 2
56	Stone.	Brick.	12 0	30 0	16 0	1 in 14	—	5 0	Unfshd.	31 19 0
57	Stone.	Brick.	18 8	30 0	18 0	1 in 18	—	5 0	—	417 13 7
58	Stone.	Brick.	48 0	30 0	18 0	1 in 30	—	6 0	—	801 12 3
59	Stone.	Brick.	42 0	30 0	18 0	1 in 20	—	6 0	—	
60	Stone.	Brick.	42 0	30 0	18 0	—	—	6 0	Unfinished	559 14 5
61	Stone.	Brick.	48 0	30 0	18 0	1 in 20	—	6 0	Unfinished	
62	Stone.	Brick.	48 0	30 0	18 0	1 in 13	—	7 0	—	988 15 11
63	Stone.	Masonry.	53 0	63 0	30 to Riv	—	—	—	—	8795 4 4
										4296 16 0

£ 99,065 11 9

Ahead and to the east, the carriages passed the stands of Newton Racecourse, partly occupied, even at this long distance, with spectators hoping to view the railway.

The Sankey Canal, the first dug in England, ran adjacent at this point, and this too was crowded with barges with full-spread sails. The viaduct above it presented one of the most difficult obstacles to the railway's progress: foundation piles were driven 30 feet into the soil, supporting a wide road 70 feet above the level of the canal with the aid of nine arches each with a 50-foot span. A guidebook, *The Stranger in Liverpool*, summed up the view before the coming of the railway:

From this spot a splendid prospect of the country is obtained, with the meanderings of the canal through a richly wooded country, where the vessels which navigate the Mersey may frequently be seen moving along the canal, impelled by the wind, apparently through fields, with all their canvases set, amidst trees and rising grounds, forming a view at once unique and picturesque.

Not for much longer.

A little to the right lay Warrington Church and the beginnings of the Warrington Junction line. The planned railway to London was designed to enter the Liverpool and Manchester route at this point, thus saving the building of fifteen miles of track. At Newton Bridge Station, roughly equidistant between Liverpool and Manchester, the fare to either place stood at 3 shillings in a closed carriage, and 2s 6d in a carriage exposed to the sparks. The little town of Newton was often thought one of the cleanest and prettiest in the country, containing Mr Boardman's farmhouse, known to date from the time of Queen Bess, and the Newton Hotel and Post Office, the finest stopover and restaurant for many miles, boasting its own bowling green. Opposite the hotel stood Wynwick Church, believed to be one of the first locations at which Christianity was introduced into Britain.

Half a mile further the trains stopped at Parkside Station to take on water. Lacey's guide contained the following recommendation:

The apparatus at which the water is supplied is worth looking at, but . . . we recommend the inspection to take place from the carriages. There are here five lines of rails, and the excitation arising from the approach of a carriage will generally so confuse a person not accustomed to walk on the railroad, as to render it almost impossible for him to discern which line it is coming on.

IT HAD BEEN A LOVELY JOURNEY, and it was time for a stretch. Earlier rain had turned to drizzle, though there was distant thunder. Some passengers still held a leaflet with the schedule for the day – the stop at Parkside was the only planned pause in the proceedings, and the travellers were 'requested not to leave their carriages'.

And so about fifty men – no women – descended from the train. Among them were Prince Esterhazy, John Calcraft MP, William Holmes MP of the Treasury, Charles Arbuthnot, Lord Gower, Lord Wilton, William Huskisson and the Mayor of Liverpool, Sir George Drinkwater. These men held the future of the world in their pocket watches: they timed their journey at 55 minutes, and they were astonished at where the railway had taken them. Even Joseph Sandars, the originator of the railway, couldn't resist the temptation to alight. It was five minutes to noon.

They milled about, looked at the sky, discussed the wonders of rail travel, stepped gingerly in the 4-foot space between the two lines. Huskisson congratulated Sandars on the completion of his wonderful project, and suggested, according to Sandars' recollection, that he must be 'one of the happiest men in the world'. William Holmes then called Huskisson away, and made a suggestion. Holmes wondered whether the day might be politically useful. The

The carriages: a mythical assemblage of class harmony.

Prime Minister seemed in good spirits, perhaps mistaking the joyous eclat for universal personal approval, and he might be willing to bury old grievances. It could be the ideal time for Huskisson to shake his hand.

Huskisson took little time to concur; for more than two years his fall out with Wellington had heckled him like a coin in a can. It was not just the confused and embarrassing nature of his departure from the cabinet that disturbed him, but the fact that he might be more influential now than ever. The newspapers reported that he had modified some of his more extreme commercial policies, and still had sufficient strength and ambition to reunite the Tories – especially, as seemed likely, as Wellington would soon be forced to step down if he continued to obstruct the demands for reform. Shortly before the opening of the railway, *The Times* noted the 'common

rumours' that Huskisson would soon be restored to the Duke of Wellington's cabinet. Failing that, he might align what remained of his party with the Whigs.

Huskisson and Wellington had seldom spoken to each other since May 1828. Politically they remained at odds on many issues, and they looked down as they passed in Westminster corridors. Socially, their relationship was a little warmer. They upheld the gentlemanly codes of the day, never letting their differences intrude on a good grouse shoot. In November 1829, Huskisson wrote to his friend Edward Littleton about encountering the Duke at the Suffolk country house of a mutual friend, Lord Hertford. As a high Tory, Hertford was also a political opponent of Huskisson's, but an old family friend. 'Some of the Whigs think my visit to Sudbury extraordinary and that I ought not to have gone. Why not? Lord Hertford . . . never allowed politics to interfere with his private friendships.' Huskisson maintained this attitude towards Wellington, although he was careful not to appear his ally. The gathering at the house was fixed for the 18th, but Huskisson postponed going to the 21st,

that I might not be considered one of the Duke's reunion – and for the same reason I staid on four days after he and his tail were gone . . . He appeared to be very well but not in good spirits. But I judge only by appearances. We shot together in the morning and I beat him at whist in the evening, with perfect good humour on both sides.

Huskisson had several names for Wellington in addition to Sir Gorgeous, and in a letter to Lord Melbourne two days before the railway opening he used another. 'The great Captain comes here tomorrow,' Huskisson wrote (Melbourne had been invited to sit alongside Huskisson in the Duke's train, but had recently undergone an operation on a carbuncle and felt unable to travel).

Great are the preparations for his reception. The feelings are not confidence in, or admiration of his political character, but rather that of awe at the man that subdued Bonaparte and forced the Catholic Question. It is the Indian worshipping the Devil because he is not conscious where he shall find a protecting deity.

In Liverpool, Huskisson had yet received no sense of the hostility awaiting Wellington at the other end of the railway.

The Duke is in his usual good luck in respect to the state of the country which he is now visiting. Nothing can be more satisfactory than the present state of manufacturing and trade, and the feeling is general that its present healthy condition is likely to be permanent. We shall see whether he takes to himself the credit of all this.

But now the Duke had witnessed his unpopularity in the streets, and he would not have been blind to Huskisson's great local approval. The shaky stature of his cabinet was reason enough for political rapprochement with an influential opponent. Lord Charles Greville, clerk of the Privy Council, had noted in his diary of 9 September:

One of the Duke's greatest misfortunes was his having no wise head to consult with in all emergencies . . . In the business of Huskisson, Huskisson himself was most anxious to have it made up, and wished Peel to speak to the Duke; but Peel would not stir . . .

But now Huskisson had his chance. He walked towards the middle carriage of his train, and approached the Duke sitting at the very front corner. Huskisson extended his hand. The Prime Minister leant over the side and shook it, and a few words of goodwill were exchanged. At this very moment, a shout went up. 'An engine is approaching. Take care, gentlemen!' Two engines had already passed the Duke's train when it was still in motion, the Phoenix and the North Star, an experience that Wellington later compared to 'the whizzing of a cannon ball'. The approaching engine was the Rocket, recognisable even from afar, its hot dirty pistons played out with cheers and gathering force in every northern playground. It was impossible to tell whether it was slowing down, but there was plenty of time to avoid it.

A CORRESPONDENT for *Blackwood's* magazine had previously noticed an interesting optical deception connected with the new locomotives.

A spectator observing their approach, when at extreme speed, can scarcely divest himself of the idea that they are . . . enlarging and increasing in size rather than moving . . . Thus an engine, as it draws near, appears to become rapidly magnified, as if it would fill up the entire space between the banks, and absorb every thing within its vortex.

As the Rocket grew nearer, the men on the track did two things: they climbed back into their carriage, or they clambered up the embankment, the safest vantage point. Their task would have been easier had the Duke's carriage been fitted with permanent steps like the others. Instead, it was thought proper that the leading car should carry a removable flight of steps suspended at the back, which could be brought at will to any part of the carriage to help women alight at their most convenient location. At this moment there was no time to fetch anything from the back. Most still managed to reach safety with ease, although some panic set in with the engine eighty feet away. Another cry went up – 'Get in! Get in!' – as Prince Esterhazy was hauled into the Duke's carriage by his hands and jacket. And then only William Holmes and William Huskisson were left on the track, in great confusion. 'Mr Huskisson . . . became flurried,' the *Liverpool Courier* reported, 'and after making two attempts to cross the road upon which the Rocket was moving, ran back, in a state of great agitation, to the side of the Duke's carriage.'

At the front of the Rocket, Joseph Locke finally saw what was happening and threw his gear lever into reverse, the only method of braking available. This process could take ten seconds to work, and he was almost upon a desperate man. Initially, Holmes and Huskisson clung on to the side of the Duke's carriage, but then panic gripped them both. This carriage was 8 feet wide, and overhung the parallel rail by two feet. Clinging on, the remaining 2-foot gap between the carriage and the advancing engine should have been just sufficient to ensure safety. But Huskisson doubted this judgement, and began to move about. He manoeuvred his good leg over the side of the carriage, but those inside failed to pull him in. Holmes cried to him by his side, 'For God's sake, Mr Huskisson, be firm!' at which point Huskisson grabbed the door of the carriage. Unable to bear his weight, the door swung wide open, suspending him directly into the path of the engine. The Rocket hit the door, and Huskisson was flung beneath its wheels.

Amid the moans and shrieks, some witnesses made mental notes.

'The engine passed over his leg and thigh, crushing it in a most frightful way,' Harriet Arbuthnot observed. She too had been talking to Huskisson just moments before the collision.

It is impossible to give an idea of the scene that followed, of the horror of everyone present or of the piercing shrieks of his unfortunate wife, who was in the car. He said scarcely more than, 'It's all over with me. Bring me my wife and let me die.'

'It is impossible to figure to one's self any event which could produce a greater sensation or be more striking to the imagination than this,' Charles Greville wrote.

The eminence of the man, the sudden conversion of a scene of gaiety and splendour into one of horror and dismay; the countless multitudes present and the effect upon them – crushed . . . in sight of his wife and at the feet (as it was) of his great political rival – all calculated to produce a deep and awful impression.

Fanny Kemble was in a following carriage, and was first made aware of an incident by a man rushing by with a speaking-trumpet, shouting orders to stop the train.

Presently a hundred voices were heard exclaiming that Mr Huskisson was killed; the confusion that ensued . . . the calling out from carriage to carriage to ascertain the truth, the contrary reports which were sent back to us, the hundred questions eagerly uttered at once, and the repeated and urgent demands for surgical assistance, created a sudden turmoil that was quite sickening.

Huskisson's friends Lord Wilton, William Rathbone and Joseph Parkes were first on the scene and were repulsed at what they saw: the wheels had passed slantingly over the calf of the leg and the middle of the thigh, crushing and tearing the muscles but leaving the knee itself uninjured – a triangular wound unfamiliar even to medical men. The upper part of the leg had a multiple fracture, and the muscles were exposed in one wet and weeping flap. Blood soaked up crushed bone like chalk powder. The arteries had not been severed, but lay flattened and pulsing in the sinewy turmoil. Observers noticed that the true pain did not encroach for almost a minute, and for a while Huskisson regarded his split limb with revulsion and astonishment as it shook beyond his control.

The news of the accident reached other travellers in other cars, and the confusion spread. 'I perceived an appearance of hustling and stooping and crowding together for which I could not well account,' wrote the man from *Blackwood's Magazine* in a watered carriage up ahead.

In another moment, a gentleman rushed forth, and came running up the line towards us; as he neared, I saw evidently that he was much agitated, and pale, and breathless – in short, that something dreadful had happened was obvious. In a state of distracted nervousness, and in broken unconnected words, he at last broke silence: 'Oh God! He is dead! He is killed! He is killed!'

'"Who? and When? and How?" burst from every mouth,' the Blackwood's correspondent continued. His first thought was that a successful attempt had been made on the Duke's life.

The truth, however, soon spread like wildfire to the right and left as it fell upon every ear like a spell. Smiles and cheerful countenances were changed for one of general gloom. Amongst those who were near the fateful spot, the first feeling was one of thankfulness, that their own immediate relative was not the victim; the next, and most permanent, was sympathy with the unhappy lady who saw her husband stretched, lacerated and bleeding on the ground.

The *Liverpool Albion* told its readers that Huskisson's right leg had been 'smashed to mummy'. There was a considerable spray of blood, though not as much as one might have expected from such an unnatural arrangement of flesh and bone beneath and above the right knee. People stood around in shock, and the first to act were the Birmingham solicitor Joseph Parkes and Lord Wilton. 'This is the death of me!' Huskisson shouted, to which Parkes replied, 'I hope not sir.' 'Yes, I am dying,' he repeated. 'Call Mrs Huskisson.'

Emily Huskisson's friends, who were endeavouring to persuade her not to go near her husband, then relented and helped her descend from the ducal car. On her approach, a man threw a coat over Huskisson's leg to save her further shock. She cried out on seeing him, a sound, according to the man from *The Times*, 'none that heard will ever forget!' She threw herself upon him in hysterics, but was held back as Lord Wilton applied a tourniquet to Huskisson's thigh, formed with handkerchiefs and a stick taken from an elderly passenger.

There was a brief consultation as to how best to remove him. A new door from a railway storeroom was wrenched from its hinges and brought to the queasy witnesses. They placed Huskisson upon it, taking particular care with his shattered leg and thigh. One of them scooped up a soft layer of detritus with his hands – a coarse and hopeless mixture of human flesh and trackside stone chippings – in the hope that it might be of some use in the hours to come. Another, in moving what remained of one limb to the board, expressed the hope that he did not add to the victim's pain. Huskisson shook his head and replied, 'This is my death,' while those close by vowed to save him. Huskisson was heard to whisper, 'God forgive me.'

There was talk of returning him to surgeons in Liverpool, but George Stephenson insisted that the Northumbrian should take him on to Manchester. The band members in the first wagon were evacuated with their instruments, and Huskisson placed flat on their platform. The engineers had just uncoupled the other wagons, with the Duke of Wellington and others still on board, when the doctors on the scene – Dr Southey, a physician to George IV and Dr Hunter, a Professor of Anatomy at Edinburgh – were joined by another, Dr Joseph Brandreth, who had rushed down from his seat behind the Phoenix.

The troubled train set off with Stephenson driving. Lord Colville supported Huskisson's head with his knee, and at the bottom of the carriage Lord Wilton held his hands and arms. His wife leaned over him with the look of someone who had seen a ghost. They tried to steady him as they set off, and to protect him against the vibration and sparks of the accelerating machine. 'In a few minutes [Huskisson] became so faint that I stopped the engine to enquire if any bleeding had taken place,' Dr Brandreth recalled. He conceived 'his speedy dissolution' to be inevitable, and suggested they stop at the first house they came to. The name of Reverend Thomas Blackburne arose, and it was resolved that they should stop at his vicarage at Eccles, some four miles before the station in Manchester.

Huskisson moaned on beneath the din of the streaming engine, itself being pushed almost beyond endurance. By one account, Huskisson's cries were steady and controlled, as if to sound otherwise would be ungentlemanly. When Joseph Brandreth told him of their plan to stop at the vicarage, he seemed to rally a little. 'Pray do so,' he told the doctor. 'I am sure my friend Blackburne will be kind to me.' In fact, unknown to the whole party, Blackburne was still at Parkside, still shocked by events.

'Upon the whole he bore the journey well,' Brandreth reported

(Dr Brandreth was the brother of the barrister Thomas Brandreth, who had built the horse-operated Cycloped at Rainhill).

We contrived a kind of fence with baize, to keep the wind from him, which blew violently, in consequence of the speed we were going . . . my medical colleagues were so uneasy at it, that I thought they would lose their self-possession.

The engine attained the speed of 35 miles per hour, which made it the fastest train in the world. Unaware of any incident, vast crowds of onlookers waved heartily as the calamity rattled past.

Thunder had caught up with them by the time they reached Eccles, and they dismounted by Eccles Bridge in a hailstorm. Lord Wilton and George Stephenson took the engine on to Manchester to obtain more specialist medical advice and wreck the mood of the expectant crowd. The remaining doctors carried Huskisson, still on his door, over a deep cutting, frequently losing their footing. The vicarage was a few hundred yards from the bridge, and the group was greeted by Mrs Blackburne, who ushered them into the front room. Huskisson was transferred to a sofa, and given brandy and laudanum as his wife grasped his hand. Dr Brandreth and Dr Hunter cut the boot and clothes from their patient's wounded leg, and found that despite its terrible appearance there was nothing about it that would prevent an operation if his strength kept up. But they faced a dilemma: 'It is a perfect mystery how the wound was produced,' Dr Brandreth noted.

The leg half way between the knee and ankle was almost entirely severed, except a small portion on the outside, but the boot was scarcely marked at all. Half way, but rather higher up, between the knee and body, the whole flesh was torn off above the broken bone, but the artery which lies over and above it was not injured . . . It is scarcely possible to understand how this could take place if the wheel had gone over him . . . or why [the engine] did not, from the enormous weight, entirely sever it.

Soon, perhaps, the surgeons would do what the Rocket failed to. It was about two o'clock. The doctors made him comfortable, but could do little more than wait for the surgeons from Manchester, who were only now being asked to bring tools for amputation.

BACK AT PARKSIDE, nothing had moved. The railway's directors, proprietors and celebrity passengers had assembled near the scene of the accident to discuss how best to proceed, and there were two lines of argument. The Duke of Wellington insisted that they all return to Liverpool, claiming that Huskisson's tragedy had cast gloom over the proceedings; above all, it would be wholly disrespectful to advance as if everything was well. The directors argued that they had a duty to prove the technical success of their grand scheme; the accident was no fault of the railway, and future travellers should not be encouraged to believe it was unsafe. Besides, there was a vast crowd at Manchester who had been waiting for hours for a glimpse of their delayed future.

As the debate continued, other passengers found their own way of passing the time. As one of them noted,

Some were in tears, some retired from the crowd and paced hastily up and down the road, some seated themselves by the side in silence. Some stood absorbed, while others discussed the accident in little knots and parties – some were gesticulating, while others were looking on speechless and motionless.

The Duke of Wellington expressed his unhappiness about proceeding to Sir Robert Peel, but his mind was changed by the arrival on horseback of civic officials from Manchester and Salford. They spoke of how the mood of the crowd was turning ugly. They feared a riot if the trains and the Duke failed to arrive. And so Wellington and his party returned to his fancy carriage, and watched as a long chain was tied to it from the engine of the Phoenix on the other line. The Phoenix and its train was then affixed to the North Star and its train, and the whole straining convoy trundled its slow pace eastwards. The man from the *Albion*, at the head of the procession, remarked how 'groups of people continued to cheer us, but we could not reply; our enjoyment was over.'

At the same time, the four Manchester surgeons – Drs Whatton, Ransome, Garside and White – arrived at Eccles by coach. They found Huskisson in great pain, and suffering from frequent spasms. These were generally so violent that their initial task was to hold down his legs and arms to prevent him falling from the couch.

William Whatton's first impression was that there had been great haemorrhaging, not only on receipt of the wound, but afterwards, from constant draining of the veins. He wrote in his notebook:

Countenance pale and ghastly, forehead covered with cold perspiration, cold and stiffened extremities, and sickness and oppression at the stomach, with frequent convulsive shudders, difficult respiration, and great constitutional alarm.

He regarded an immediate amputation highly desirable, but considered such an act 'madness' in Huskisson's present state, resulting in certain death. He and his colleagues attempted to restore his health with warm cordials and more laudanum, and by applying hot water to his hands, feet and the side of his chest it was hoped that he would improve sufficiently to endure the shock of an operation.

AMPUTATION was the dynamic medical topic of the day, and important advances had recently been made in severance of all kinds: the Napoleonic Wars had provided much experience of thigh, leg, wrist, fingers, hip and shoulder. In the middle of September 1830,

William Lawrence, a surgeon at St Bartholomew's Hospital in East London, delivered a lecture about the latest advances. Two methods were considered – the circular incision and the flap operation (a third, the rough or hacking incision, was now out of favour, regarded as too crude, or for field emergencies only). The circular incision, a three-stage method whereby a circular cut in the soft parts surrounding the bone may be precisely joined to heal after the removal of the offending limb, was preferable for the amputation of the upper leg and thigh.

'Generally speaking,' Lawrence told his audience of surgeons and students,

the rule of proceeding is to amputate the limb so as to preserve as much of it as we can, without leaving any of the disease that requires the operation. Then we have to consider the proceedings that are necessary in order to arrest the haemorrhage, the mode of performing it in the quickest manner [and] the steps which are subsequently needed for preventing future haemorrhage, by securing the orifices of the divided vessels, the mode of uniting the wound, and the treatment of the patient after the operation has been performed.

Dr Lawrence demonstrated each stage of the operation with the aid of a cadaver on a table in front of him.

The first step was to apply the tourniquet. Bleeding could be stopped by tying any circular bandage around the limb with a certain degree of force, although a genuine tourniquet was preferable: with this instrument a girth is buckled around the limb with the aid of a pad and a tightening screw, thus ensuring a certain amount of movement along a leg and a variation of pressure. In ideal circumstances, the pad should be placed directly on the artery.

The second stage should ensure that the incision into the soft parts leaves adequate flesh to cover the wound even after the inevitable contraction that will occur in the skin and muscles after cutting. The object is to saw through the bone as high up as possible, in order to ensure an adequate covering of the soft parts over the stump. The last step is to saw through the bone, ideally with the help of a retractor, a stiff piece of linen divided at one end into two strips and wrapped either side of the bone, so that an assistant can hold it clear of the soft parts and limit the risk of accidental mis-sawing.

The rest is mopping up: tying the arteries and other vessels, gradually loosening the tourniquet, securing any bleeding lesions with ligatures. Great care should be taken with this process, for, as Dr Lawrence observed wearily from his own experience,

it is a very perplexing circumstance to have haemorrhage occur after the operation – to be called to the patient in the evening or the night after the operation, and to be obliged to undo the dressing of the stump in consequence of the bleeding. It is very painful to the patient, and very inconvenient to the surgeon.

Finally, the dressing of the wound: cold water applied to the stump usually checked the bleeding from any small vessels; it was then safe to apply strips of sticking plaster over the stump; the old method of applying a woollen cap over the end was discouraged, as this usually delayed the healing process and encouraged inflammation.

Dr Lawrence then set to work on other parts of the body in front of him: the fingers, the wrist joint, the hip joint. It was clear from his manner that he was a leader in his field. It was a shame, therefore, that he was sharing the benefit of his experience at a teaching hospital in London on the very day that he was needed 200 miles away in the front room of a vicarage in Eccles.

A T ABOUT FOUR O'CLOCK Huskisson gained enough strength to conduct some business: he wished to add a codicil to his will. He had discussed this amendment with his secretary William Wainewright just the night before, a deed that suggested premonition. Wainewright was already present at the vicarage, and recalled how Huskisson had told him the previous evening, 'What would I give to have the next fifteen hours over!'

He dictated the private amendment, a simple matter by which his wife would inherit any property that had become his since his last will was composed in 1827, and managed to sign his name. 'I have seen that signature,' a man from *The Times* reported a day later,

and have also compared it to a frank given by Mr Huskisson some short time before. The direction on the frank is in a sloping, fluent, easy hand: that of last night's signature, though the formation of the letters is essentially the same, is more upright and betrays great nervous compression. After he had written 'W Huskisson' and had given the paper to Mr Wainewright, he called for it again, for the purpose of placing his usual dot between the W and H, – a circumstance which proves that to the very last he retained his partiality for all the minuteness of business.

The signature became a serious attraction. It was later seen by a man from the *Chronicle*, who also compared it with a less stressful version. 'I am competent to announce how near it resembled his customary way of writing,' he concluded. 'The formation of all the letters is essentially the same – particularly the capital H, although it is easy to see how shaken the hand must have been that wrote it.'

Huskisson then requested the sacrament, and he read the Lord's Prayer with Lord Wilton. According to Dr Brandreth,

as he came to the part 'Forgive us our trespasses', he said, 'I hope I have no enemy in the world. I am sure I have no enmity to any human being.' He never once alluded to the accident.

The spasms increased their frequency and violence, and Huskisson 'could not refrain from crying out, praying to be released, and asking how long it would last.'

In his despair he heard distant cannon fire, and was told that it marked the Duke of Wellington's arrival in Manchester. According to Charles Greville, Huskisson said feebly, 'I hope to God the Duke may get safe through the day'.

As it was, Wellington was facing anguish of his own. The trip to Manchester continued to elicit excitement from onlookers despite the great delay; even on its first journey, a late passenger train was not considered unusual. At the twenty-fifth milepost the expedition met George Stephenson returning with the Northumbrian. He was inundated with questions, and told the crowd what he knew of Huskisson's health, though the news was two hours stale. He could not suppress his own contribution to the rescue mission, claiming that his steam engine had set a new record for speed. He again affixed the Northumbrian to the Duke's carriages, and having already reversed the gear to stop, set off at a great speed again towards Manchester.

As Wellington had feared, the reaction to their arrival was mixed. Some cheered, but there were others – many of them weavers – who hissed and threw vegetables. There were two *tricoleur* flags hoisted, and banners advocating 'Vote by Ballot' and 'No Corn Laws!'. Passengers disembarked shortly before 3 p.m., many heading straight to the cold meats laid out in the company's warehouse. Fearing attack, Wellington remained in his tented vehicle as food was brought in, and requested that the engines be made ready for a swift return to Liverpool. His travelling companions included Reverend Blackburne, who only now learnt that Huskisson had been delivered to his vicarage. He rushed home at once by horse carriage.

The journey back was more tortuous still. Only the Duke's carriages and two others made the journey without incident, departing at 4.30 and dismounting some two hours later (the hero of Waterloo got off at Roby, and returned to the Marquis of Salisbury's home at Childwall to avoid further risk). Twenty-four other carriages faced further delays – a farcical combination of displaced engines, failing power and the lack of turning spaces. Three of the eight engines pulled the remaining cars in one tiring line, many lashed together with rope. In the midst of them was Charles Vignoles, who noted in his diary that he had found yet another reason to distrust George Stephenson. 'We crept on at only snail's pace,' he wrote, observing how their new speed of 5 miles an hour was the equivalent of a brisk walk. He described further reasons for delay – a large crowd of people happily walking over the rails, and the condition of the rails themselves, which he found to be encrusted with gravel and mud.

When darkness fell at seven the convoy was still not halfway. Inevitably, it started to rain again. At Eccles the trains stopped to inquire about Huskisson, and passengers learnt that he was looking frail, and that an amputation was thought unlikely. They set off again, although they wouldn't see Liverpool until 10 p.m. (Fanny Kemble, ecstatic no more, had plumped for the easy option, accepting, with her relieved mother, a coach ride back to a nearby country estate from a friend.)

The journey slowed further in the darkness, the drivers fearful of the unknown. The crowds dispersed slowly, and some drunks, who had enjoyed the refreshment booths since morning, held up candles to see the travellers on their way. Others had a more malicious intent: the returning Comet, leading the procession with its driver clutching fiery tarred rope to light the way, crashed into a wheelbarrow, seemingly placed on the rails to obstruct it. And from several bridges the trains were pelted with missiles.

Not long after reaching Parkside, the passengers saw in the gloom a uniformed group of men carrying tools alongside the rails. In fact these were disgruntled bandsmen with their instruments, recently convinced that they had been forgotten; there had been no room for them on the carriages that had gone by with the Duke of Wellington, and their own flat wagon, the one that carried Huskisson to Eccles, appeared to have been lost. They trudged home by the side of the tracks, along grass that was rapidly turning to mud.

At the start of the railway in Liverpool another unfamiliar story was unfolding. Much earlier in the day, not long after dawn, a small group of men had each paid a railway worker two shillings to obtain one of the best views of the opening ceremony from a circular chimney on the roof of the large tunnel entrance. They were hoisted up by rope and board, and no doubt enjoyed the spectacle until it was time to descend. But by then the person who had helped them up was nowhere to be found, and they were getting wet and hungry. At about 8 p.m. one of them came up with a solution. John Harrison, a professor of gymnastics and swordsmanship at the gym in Colquitt Street, managed to lower himself down a rope hand over hand, and instructed the others to copy his technique. Then they went looking for the railway worker.

At the vicarage, the news had not improved. 'It was now evident that there was no chance,' Dr Brandreth remembered,

and I thought it our duty to tell Mrs Huskisson. Till this moment all that she had feared was the amputation of the limb. Mr H from the first was convinced that the accident would be fatal, and never entertained the slightest hope . . . We had a dreadful scene with Mrs Huskisson, of course out of the room, but at last she calmed herself and during the rest of the time sat weeping by his couch.

Between spasms, Huskisson talked to those around him. To Brandreth he said, 'You see I shall never live to make any return for your kindness. You have done all that is possible, but it is all in vain.' A while later, after more laudanum, he said: 'Why endeavour to support my strength? I must die, it is only prolonging my sufferings.'

AT 9 P.M., two hours later than scheduled, twenty people sat down to dinner at Liverpool's Adelphi Hotel. James Radley had sold sixty advance tickets for the celebration in aid of 'the success and promotion of steam power', and had prepared food for 230, but most were still struggling back on the moonlit railway. The band was informed that their services would not be required. William Brown, the prominent local merchant who was chairman for the evening, was presumed to be in a forlorn carriage somewhere in the rain, so his place was taken by another businessman, John Ashton Yates. An elaborate dinner of turtle, Dee salmon, stewed partridges and roast black game was consumed in subdued mood as conflicting news of William Huskisson arrived between courses. It was announced that amputation had been performed, and that the patient had lived, and that all was to be well. Towards the dessert, a new arrival straight from the track revealed there had been no operation, and their MP was fading.

By 11 p.m. accurate news was still hours away. The first toast was to the King, and then to Huskisson: 'May his sufferings be speedily assuaged, and his health restored.' A rally of toasts followed to absent friends – to the Duke of Wellington, George Stephenson – and a few to those in attendance – Captain Ericsson, John Braithwaite, Charles Vignoles – and fulsome speeches then embraced the progress of steam in America. It was estimated that twenty Americans had travelled to witness the day's opening, among them Francis B Ogden, the United States Consul, the first person to successfully navigate a vessel at sea by steam, a journey that had survived a gale and had since been repeated many times.

Ogden was praised by J C Robertson, the editor of the *Mechanics' Magazine*, who announced that the success of the Liverpool and Manchester Railway would soon be equalled by an even more ambitious project taking shape in the United States, the Baltimore and Ohio Railroad, which, though far from completion, would one day stretch between two and three hundred miles. Great applause followed, after which Ogden attempted to provide more details. Between twenty and thirty miles had already been completed, ninety more miles were in progress, and the whole project could be completed within three years. But this was only the start: he mentioned an order from Louisiana for British rails for another extensive line from New Orleans to Lake Erie. He was sure that the directors of this line would order engines designed by Braithwaite and Ericsson. He was nervous that squabbling between individual states would delay the progress of future lines. He sat down to a clatter of noise, a mixture of cheering and awesome gossip about the potential of steam travel to transform their world. There was no more news of Huskisson, good or bad.

I N FACT, Huskisson was already dead. At the same time as the dinner was breaking up, William Wainewright sat in the vicarage study at Eccles and gathered himself to write a letter to the Mayor of Liverpool.

Sir,
    With the deepest grief, I have to acquaint you, for the information of yourself, and of the community over which you preside, that Mr Huskisson breathed his last at 9 o'clock this evening. He was attended from the moment of the accident, with indefatigable assiduity, by Dr Brandreth of Liverpool, Dr Hunter of Edinburgh, and Mr Ransome, Mr Whatton, Mr Garside and Mr White, of Manchester.
    His last moments were soothed by the devoted attentions of his now distracted widow, and by the presence of some of his distinguished and faithful friends.
    I have the honour to be, Sir,
    Your most obedient humble servant.

    At 7.30 the following morning the Duke of Wellington composed a note to Liverpool's mayor.

Sir,
    I enclose a note received about an hour ago, from Lord Wilton, which will make you acquainted with the melancholy result of the misfortune of yesterday. [The note has since been lost.]
    Having all been witnesses of this misfortune, and as all must feel for the loss which the public, and the town of Liverpool in particular, have

sustained in Mr Huskisson, I do not think that it would be satisfactory to any, that there should be at this moment in the town any parade or festivity.

Under these circumstances I propose not to visit the town this morning, and I request you to excuse me for declining to dine with the corporation this day.

I likewise beg leave to suggest to you the expediency of postponing to some future period the ceremony of your delivering to me the freedom of your corporation, to which you did me the honour of admitting me some time ago.

I have the honour to be, Sir,

Your most obedient humble servant,

WELLINGTON

At the dawn of the railway age, even bad news still travelled slowly. Many shops failed to open, and shutters remained drawn on private houses. But in the docks there was gaiety: unaware of the fatality, the ships were rigged out in bright streamers, and there was noise from steam hooters. They were still expecting the Duke's visit.

The businessman Sir James Carnegie also had an altered diary. That morning he was due to meet Huskisson to settle the details of his new steam navigation company, a further effect of the increased trade expected from the new railway. His company was set to employ a regular line of steam vessels between Liverpool and America, and between London and Bordeaux, Lisbon and Gibraltar. Huskisson was believed to have been a great supporter of the scheme.

'I cannot describe to you the horror and grief of everybody here,' Mrs Thomas Fletcher, a relative of Henry Booth, wrote from Liverpool that morning to her sister in London.

Our member, a man beloved by all parties, looked up to by the nation . . . everything conspires to render the blow shocking and awful. Nothing is spoken of today but this. Every face wears a settled gloom . . . Is it not surprising that Mr Huskisson should have gone into a situation where there was a possibility of danger, and more especially when he was delicate, and one leg numb since his last illness? I would send you a Liverpool paper today, but the edition is all sold up.

Not long after cancelling his engagements, the Duke of Wellington received the following account of the accident from Dr Whatton.

My Lord Duke,

As one of the surgeons in attendance upon the Rt Hon Gentleman, I therefore have the honour of addressing your grace . . . In consequence of loss of blood, and from the shock sustained by the constitution, the greatest depression of the powers of life ensued, followed by cold faintings and the most violent spasms . . . It was not possible under so severe a shock upon the nervous system to recruit his strength . . .

I do not learn that this melancholy occurrence took place from any neglect or carelessness of the engineers, or of any person entrusted with the management of the carriages, but rather from the want of caution and knowledge of the machines on the part of the Rt Hon Gentleman himself.

The question of blame was a feature of the inquest, organised with great speed that same morning. A jury began assembling at the Grapes Public House in Eccles at 9 a.m., although the coroner, Mr Milne, didn't appear until ten. He was in a hurry: he had another inquest at Flixton at one o'clock, and yet another in Manchester after that, but his desire to proceed was delayed by the absence of the Earl of Wilton, a principal witness. He sent the jury to view the corpse at the vicarage.

There they met a further delay, owing to Emily Huskisson's insistence that she stay alone with the body as long as possible. Her husband now lay in an upstairs bedroom, having been moved from the front room shortly after death. After she had been forcibly persuaded to leave, the jury went in two or three at a time so that their footsteps did not add to Mrs Huskisson's grief, and they lifted a cold sheet for a moment to view the damage. Lord Granville wrote later that they barely examined the wounds at all.

The Earl of Wilton arrived at the Grapes shortly after noon, and replayed the details once more. Then Lord Granville explained that at the time of the accident Huskisson was still suffering from a numbness in his leg from a previous operation, and that this probably contributed to the slow pace of his movements. Neither Wilton nor Granville could remember the raising of any coloured signal flags from the Rocket or any other engine. At the close, the coroner addressed a few words to the jury, who lost no time in returning a verdict of accidental death. They purposely acquitted the railway's directors, engineers and machinery of all blame. The coroner's official report announced that no 'deodand' had been attached to the Rocket, a traditional sentence after fatal events whereby the physical cause of an accident is offered up to God as a sacrifice, and as an apology, before being destroyed.

Not long after the inquest had broken up, differing opinions were being expressed in private correspondence. One eye-witness, Lady Frances Sandon, wrote to a friend:

I am afraid there was some degree [of] blame attached to the Director of the Carriage [Locke], who it is thought ought not to have gone at such a pace where the crowd was so great around the carriages.

Another letter, written by the MP Edward Littleton, Mrs Huskisson's host in Staffordshire after her husband's death, suggested yet another interpretation. 'I was present with him from the moment he entered the car till that of the accident,' he wrote to Lord Palmerston, enclosing his own illustration of the collison. He was among the fifty men walking around during the water stop at Parkside. On seeing the approaching engine,

everyone entered as soon as they could, or stood still between the cars – I had just time to enter through the wicket [carriage door] . . . Everyone was getting in or into a place of safety to allow the engine to pass, when the Duke, observing a stir said (I was close by and heard it): 'We seem to be going on – you had better step in'!!! Had Huskisson stood where he was he would have been safe. The Duke's last words were, accidentally, the cause of his misfortune.

The inquest failed to mention one further feature of the accident. In Huskisson's jacket pocket at the time of the collision were two speeches, both to be delivered that evening, both rescued as rigor mortis set in. One carried the instruction 'to be burnt at my death' but since these were among the last words that her husband ever wrote, Mrs Huskisson couldn't bring herself to do it.

Both addresses were to be delivered at celebratory dinners after the triumphant return from Manchester. One was a brief tribute to James Watt, written in an expansive script on four sheets of square paper. According to the notes that accompany the address, probably written by Mrs Huskisson, the words were written at one o'clock in the morning on the 15th.

'The Chairman has permitted me to propose to you one Toast, which will require, I am sure, but a very short introduction to recommend it to your favourable reception,' Huskisson had written in a rushed hand.

On this day, on this occasion, and on this meeting . . . we must not forget the triumphs of Science and the glory of Peace. We must not forget how greatly this our Country, and this part of the country more particularly, is indebted to the transcendent genius and practical discoveries of the modest benefactor of Mankind. Gentlemen, when you contemplate the wonderful effects produced by the . . . organised power of steam, I need not more particularly point to the immortal inventions of James Watt.

It has been said by an eloquent writer that the history of his life is the proudest proof of the dominion of mind over matter . . . The services of Mr Watt, Gentlemen, embrace too wide a field to be entered upon on this occasion. His fame is not a sudden blaze, dazzling and confounding by its vivid but transitory splendour. It is rather that greatest warmth and growing light which, progressively expanding like the eternal sun, spreads new life over the face of nature, holding out the prospects of a rich harvest to the industry of all the inhabitants of the earth.

Gentlemen, our tribute can add nothing to fame like this, but in marking our respect for his memory we shall discharge a debt of gratitude which we must all feel at the present moment.

His second speech was longer and more self-serving, but unnervingly poignant. It began by acknowledging 'the success of the spirited undertaking' which his anticipated audience had all gathered to celebrate. He called the railway a bold endeavour, one which not only 'dissipates the doubts of the sceptic and converts the incredulous, but surpasses . . . the most sanguine expectations of its early proprietors and most ardent friends.'

. . . From the first I was a warm but disinterested advocate for the present great experiment. Now that it has been made, and difficulties of no ordinary nature overcome, I may be permitted to look back with satisfaction to the humble but zealous part I took in first promoting the attempt. I speak now of 1825. From the official situation which I then held as a Minister of the Crown as President of the Board of Trade, I was not at liberty, according to Parliamentary usage, to take a part in what is considered the private business of the House, but I felt that the application to Parliament for this Railway, though technically a private petition, involved great public interests – those interests which it is the special duty of the Board of Trade to countenance and encourage, and avowedly on this ground not consider it inconsistent with my character of a Minister . . . I felt it my bounden duty to give my strenuous support to the principle of the Bill on its second reading in the House of Commons . . .

Gentlemen, I have said that I considered that in this private undertaking were involved great public interests. Need I in the present state of the Commerce of this Country, specify what these interests are? Most of those who hear me know well with what difficulties we have to struggle in maintaining a successful competition with foreign rivals. They know well that it can only be maintained by incessant industry, by unwearied diligence, by constantly increasing skill in our manufacturing population; but they know well that all their efforts would be unavailing without the greatest economy not of money only but of time, in all the operations of trade. It is in this point of view that Railways will be found invaluable – increased facility and security of transport, increased dispatch, and diminished expense will keep the balance even with our foreign rivals, if not turn it in our favour, and will bring the conveniences and comforts of life cheapened more readily to the door of every consumer in these kingdoms. In short, the principle of a Railway is that of commerce itself – it multiplies the enjoyment of Mankind by increasing the facilities and diminishing the labour by which the means of those enjoyments are produced and distributed throughout the world.

Huskisson concluded with a look to the future, and the new railways that would link the great manufacturing districts to London, and he saw only benefits. This progress he likened to 'the increased velocity of a projectile'. He then thanked his anticipated audience for the great friendship they had shown him on his recent visits, after which he probably entertained some thought of sitting down amidst a sea of applause.

Of course, the speech was only ever read in private. On the afternoon after it was discovered, the Liverpool and Manchester Railway began operating with 130 people aboard. It was one of very few public services not disrupted by Huskisson's death.

T HE OBITUARIES in the newspapers were not perfunctory affairs. *The Times* wrote of someone who seldom uttered what was not worthy of attention, and of a man possessed of 'a powerful and protecting authority . . . one whose knowledge was conversant with realities – whose reasonings on matters of political economy and on finance might be taken for a manual'.

The Times assessed, and generally acclaimed, his contribution to free trade and British shipping interests, and his opening up of the silk trade. In all cases, the public had benefited from lower prices and greater choices, and one day they would forget to thank him for it.

Mr Huskisson's services to the nation . . . no man of the present age has presided with anything like equal credit to himself, or solid utility to the public . . . Report says that he, and certain others of the same views on foreign and domestic policy, were soon to have been announced as members of the Duke of Wellington's cabinet. We neither confirm nor deny that rumour. The loss . . . of such a man, so enlightened in his opinions, and so practised in affairs, must at such a time be irreparable.

Charles Greville wrote in his diary that it was remarkable that it was only within the last five or six years that he acquired the great reputation which he latterly enjoyed.

I do not think that he was looked upon as more than a second-rate man till his speeches on the silk trade and the shipping interest; but when he became President of the Board of Trade he devoted himself with indefatigable application to the maturing and reducing to practice those commercial improvements with which his name is associated, and to which he owes all of his glory and most of his unpopularity.

Greville praised his abilities but questioned his judgement, particularly in joining Wellington's government on Goderich's resignation, and his speech afterwards at Liverpool regarding the Corn Laws, and of course his calamitous quarrel regarding his departure. As to the Duke, Greville spoke portentously of how it was 'perilous to cross his path'. Of all the thousands at the opening of the railway,

one man only is killed, and that man is the most dangerous political opponent, the one from who he had most to fear. It is the more remarkable because these great people are generally taken such care of, and put out of the chance of accidents. Canning had scarcely reached the zenith of his power when he was swept away, and the field was left open to the Duke, and no sooner is he reduced to a state of danger and difficulty than the ablest of his adversaries is removed by a chance beyond all power of calculation.

The *Spectator* judged Huskisson 'in many respects the most remarkable person that Parliament had to boast,' all the more outstanding because he was sprung from humble parents,

without fortune, without rank, neither supported by powerful friends nor pushed forward by secret influence . . . He did not sacrifice his principles, though they were such as rendered him little acceptable to the great; and yet, such was the singular force of his exalted intellect, and so effectually did it enable him to command the attention and respect of all that he approached, that even his honesty did not impede his rise.

The magazine judged that no parliamentarian of recent memory, not even George Canning, ever commanded the respect of his colleagues like the MP for Liverpool. 'He convinced or he silenced, but he never irritated. He seldom uttered an ill-natured word, because he was seldom influenced by an ill-natured feeling.' Domestically, he was considered amiable and virtuous.

The same simplicity and kindness and integrity which formed the charm of the member of the Legislature, shed their hallowed influences around the fireside circle of the private citizen. Such was William Huskisson on Wednesday morning; and on Wednesday night, all that remained of the glory of the Senate, the delight of his acquaintance, the idol of his family, was a mass of mouldering clay – to which 'the worm was a sister, and the slow-worm a brother and a kinsman!'

The Liverpool newspapers judged Huskisson's death a great local and personal tragedy, and that it was. In so far as it was also a national one, its tragic elements were traditional: a protagonist falling from high office; a figure seen off by his own actions. The *Liverpool Journal* summoned up Cicero for its conclusion that

Huskisson 'could afford to die, much better than we could afford to lose him'.

More than this, his death was a powerful symbol: nothing could obstruct a machine that promised to re-lay the old landed certainties. Of all the great reforms that bound the middle of the nineteenth century – electoral reform, the repeal of the Corn Laws, the health and employment laws – the first of them was a revolution in personal communication that began in earnest in Liverpool in September 1830. The railway ended parochialism; the hundreds of thousands who now passed through Newton would finally see for themselves the absurdity of that tiny village sending two representatives to Westminster while their destination sent none.

Huskisson's death brought the opening of the railway to a far wider audience than would have otherwise observed it, for even the greatest of technological feats fared less well in the drinking houses than tales of bloody demise. Simultaneously, the true worth of the day filtered down – a person could travel thirty miles in less time than it took to eat a meal.

WHEN HUSKISSON'S BODY left the vicarage at Eccles on the 18th, it travelled not by rail but conventional means. He was laid in his coffin shortly before midnight on Friday, the brass plate still rough with shavings. The inscription bore nothing sentimental:

The Right Honourable W Huskisson.
Died 15th September, in the 61st year of his age.
AD 1830

John Bradburn completed his duties and covered the body in black silk, and prepared his colleagues to place the coffin straight in the hearse that had been waiting outside since late afternoon. Mrs

Huskisson's grief forced an alternative. She found it impossible to leave her husband that evening to return to Staffordshire, and spent another night close to him at Eccles.

The following morning, still in an agitated state, she left in a carriage with all the blinds drawn. The coffin made its slow way in another direction, passing bowed villagers and muffled peals, and changing horses only at the quietest inns to avoid attention. The procession reached Warrington at 3 p.m., and the trail of mourners grew steadily until it reached Liverpool five hours later; at the end there were more than ten carriages and at least 500 had joined the bleak parade. There was quite a crowd when the coffin slid into the Town Hall, though its arrival had been unannounced.

The funeral plans, which shut the town.

THE DAY BEFORE THE FUNERAL, with almost all the arrangements in place, the directors of the railway held an energetic discussion concerning the morality of running their trains on Sundays. Two of them insisted that no one should have any need for travel on the Lord's day, and that they would feel uneasy about employing non-religious men to operate the engines and receive payment from these actions. Others argued that only those who had critical work on a Sunday should be allowed to travel, as opposed to those with pleasurable aims, but they were unable to provide a method whereby such stipulation could be tested. At the vote it was decided that the railway would run on a Sunday, but only outside church hours, at which point the two orthodox directors resigned, and sold their shares at a profit of £95 each.

At the same time, an intriguing letter appeared in the *Albion* suggesting the railway carriages had a fundamental design flaw that had contributed to Huskisson's death. 'Gentlemen,' began the correspondent, RT,

You ought, forthwith, to make every door of every one of your railway carriages to open INWARDS; I mean INTO, and not OUT of the carriage as they do at present. The importance of this is too evident, after the late shocking catastrophe, to be denied or disputed.

RT had other schemes: to limit each carriage to one door each, and to have this placed as far as possible from the engines running on other rails (he relented in a postscript that two doors may be necessary to enable two-way travel, but pleaded that the 'dangerous door' be locked. The writer apologised for the didactic style, but 'I do not approve of people's bones being crushed and Juggernauted if it can be avoided.'

Huskisson's obituary in *The Times* was accompanied by another practical idea from a reader.

The plan . . . consists in causing two wheels, which may be called feeler-wheels, to run on the rail about 20 feet ahead of the locomotive engine, and attached to the engine by very simple machinery, in such manner that any obstacle on the rail liable to do mischief would, through the medium of the feeler-wheels, put a drag on the carriage sufficient to check its dangerous velocity, or to stop it altogether, before it could arrive at the obstacle.

The directors' response to this suggestion was not recorded.

HUSKISSON'S FUNERAL began shortly after ten o'clock on the morning of Friday 24 September. Liverpool closed for the occasion, and almost 50,000 people saw the coffin pass from its resting place at the Town Hall along Castle Street, Lord Street, Church Street, Bold Street, Slater Street and Duke Street, to its final home in an iron-lined grave at the end of Hope Street.

Those not in the procession had gathered since daybreak at good spots along the route, as many had done nine days earlier in happier mood. A slipway of iron barriers had been erected along the entire length of the journey to hold back the crowds, a grey strip of parallel rails that might have been lifted directly from Edge Hill or Chat Moss. Viewed from the top of the Adelphi Hotel, the portioned streets resembled an urban racecourse, albeit one at which all the spectators had just heard that their fancied horse had lost. Indeed, many in the crowd had returned the day before from the St Leger at Doncaster.

The large turn-out had been expected. The organising committee had held meetings with local constables, and two schemes emerged to maintain decorum. Those who wanted to join the procession had to submit their names in writing to the committee at the Town Hall, but when time made this impracticable, placards went up stating that anyone in mourning dress would be accepted in the cortege. A ticket system was established for the burial service, with different colours admitting holders to different sections of St James's Cemetery. These were made available at the new Court House on the Wednesday and Thursday, but only between 1 p.m.

and 3 p.m. each day; vast queues and crushes accompanied the distribution of 3,000 tickets.

The funeral committee also met with Mrs Huskisson, who had only agreed to his burial in Liverpool with great reluctance. She had set her heart on a small service at home in Eartham, and had changed her mind only when visited at the vicarage in Eccles two days after the accident. Lord Granville, accompanied by a delegation of Liverpool churchmen, presented a petition signed by 264 dignatories and merchants, all

requesting that his remains may be interred within the precincts of this town, in which his distinguished public worth and private virtue secured for him the respect and esteem of the whole community.

She remained adamant that she wanted no pomp or parade: she had refused the Mayor's request that her husband's body should lie in state, and had declined the offer of mass gun salutes. But she couldn't limit the genuine outpouring of sympathy from the local inhabitants, most of whom had never seen their representative in person, but all of whom had been aghast at reports of his extinction. Women filled all available space in residential windows, and young men clambered on trees and roofs for a better view. Their clothes were soaking, for rain and hail had fallen since dawn. It was only when the coffin began its shouldered skulk through the cemetery that the sky cleared a little and a low sun emerged to hurt their eyes.

The order of procession was precise. The coffin, draped in a velvet pall on a trestle table and covered with plumes of feathers, was visited by a stream of mourners between 9 and 10 a.m., their path through the Town Hall guided by a phalanx of what were still called truncheon men. Two mutes, who stood at the head and foot of the coffin, then led the grieving out of the hall, and climbed upon horses. They were followed by 1,100 mourners who joined from the street, and a strict formation was observed: the mourners, six abreast, were joined by members of the funeral committee (four abreast in their scarves and hatbands), twenty-eight local clergymen, two more mutes, the Reverend Blackburne and Dr Brandreth. Then came the pall bearers in their own carriages: Lord Gower, Sir John Tobin, Lord Stanley, Charles Lawrence and others, followed by two more mutes. Then came Huskisson in a hearse. The body was followed by the chief mourners, including Huskisson's two surviving brothers, and Lord Granville, Lord Colville and Mr Wainewright. After them, a further trampling of 900 locals but no more mutes.

The cortege lasted 2,000 yards and moved to the sound of muffled church bells. Delighted schoolchildren were brought from their classes to see what they could. The windows of all the houses were filled with spectators, although the home of John Bolton in Duke Street was an exception, its blinds drawn close as if the house itself had died. It had been fourteen days since Huskisson had arrived in town.

Mrs Huskisson was too griefstricken to attend any part of the ordeal, and remained at the home of Edward Littleton and family ('She is in the profoundest affliction,' Littleton informed the Marquess of Anglesey). Despite her wishes, cannons went off all over town. A 32-pounder announced that the coffin had left the Town Hall, a few smaller guns fired along the route, and when the coffin entered the gates of the cemetery a brass 6-pounder alerted the town that the burial service had begun. At this point, the end of the trail of mourners was still two streets away, for the procession measured almost half a mile.

The service in the small Greek temple in the cemetery's valley was conducted by the Rector Jonathan Brooks, the lesson and psalms taking fifteen minutes. Many of those left outside had time to look around. A public subscription of £20,000 had funded the design and sculpture of this land on the site of an old quarry, its stone already visible on many public buildings and the local docks. The cemetery was distinguished principally by its 105 ornamental catacombs and the classical design of its chapel, the latter built close to the site of a seventeenth-century windmill. The burial site comprised 44,000 square yards of diggable land, surrounded by stone walls and elegant railings. Huskisson was being interred near the centre, almost opposite a street that had previously received his name but had not yet been completed.

The intimate cortege moved from the chapel to the grave, and weeping could be heard for the first time, not least from Captain Thomas Huskisson, William's half-brother, whom he had appointed paymaster of the navy, and Major Samuel Huskisson, the oldest brother. Observing the latter, a man from the *Liverpool Courier* made a note in his book: 'His fast-flowing tears bedewing the grave of his departed brother during the whole of this last mournful scene.'

The iron chamber into which the coffin was lowered was designed to protect it from the shifting ground. The first inches of earth were pitched on top with shovels; by the next day there would be eight feet of it. Those who had attended wrote their accounts in diaries and letters, and a man from *The Times* dispatched his observations to London on a four-horse carriage:

I have seen more than one public funeral, and I know something of the gorgeous pageantry so lavishly displayed in the burials of our Monarchs; but though I saw the ashes of Grattan and Canning deposited in one of the most august of Christian temples amid the vain regrets of men the most distinguished for rank, talent and genius, and though the interment of Royalty takes hold upon the imagination from its necessary connection with the most sumptuous display of human pomp and greatness, I have never witnessed any spectacle so impressive as the appearance of this vast multitude, standing erect under the open canopy of Heaven, and joining in one spontaneous tribute of respect to the memory of their late Representative.

The local press was there in proud numbers, and had their own frank impressions; their man had grown in stature in the last few days, grown even since the obituaries:

Today his mangled body was committed to the silent tomb, amidst the heartfelt anguish of his sorrowing relatives, and the tears of countless thousands . . . How impressive the voice which issues from Mr Huskisson's tomb! 'All men think all men mortal but themselves'. But the death of this celebrated man, which was as tragical as it was sudden, shows the futility of this vain conceit.

An editorial in the *Liverpool Courier* began to consider a suitable replacement in Parliament. Only one candidate had declared himself, William Ewart, but other names under consideration included John Gladstone and Sir Robert Peel. A tricky job, for Huskisson was now considered 'the hope of his country and the friend of mankind'. He died

at a time when the prospect of an extended sphere of usefulness in the exercise of his eminent abilities drew upon him the eyes of all the nation. A few short days ago he was surrounded by the throng of admiring friends, who received the pledge of friendship from that hand which, alas!, ere the sun revolved, was unstrung and cold in the merciless grasp of death.

The Manchester papers would not be outdone. The *Courier* wrote of the great decorum observed throughout the morning – no drunkards, no arrests. The report was carried on the same page as news of the death of the libertarian essayist William Hazlitt (fittingly, in *The Spirit Of The Age*, Hazlitt attacked the regressive values of one of Huskisson's high Tory opponents, Lord Eldon).

The newspaper also carried plans for further railways. It was hoped that in three years a fractured line would run from Preston to London, a 200-mile journey that would take only eight hours. The proposed route was far from direct, and reflected the growing complexity of the planned railway system: passengers would travel from

Preston to Newton via Wigan, change to the Warrington Branch Company for the train to Nantwich, change again for the Liverpool and Birmingham Company, and then speed to London from Birmingham. The capital required for building all four lines was already in place.

The experience of the Liverpool and Manchester line suggested that these routes would have a damaging effect on the road-bound coach trade. For the impact of the railway was immediate: stage coaches were travelling between the two towns relatively empty, and the fares were reduced, so that an outside trip now cost 4 shillings, not seven. In contrast, the new railway was running consistently full. It ran five times a day in each direction, three engines doing the journey in under two hours at the cost of 7 shillings, and two managing it in three hours at a cost of 4 shillings. In the first week of operation 6,104 passengers took the journey, or 763 per day. The receipts were £2,034 and 11 shillings. Reassured that Huskisson's accident was unique, the numbers increased as the week drew on. The inns at each end of the journey found they could greatly boost their trade by providing free transfers from the platforms.

Huskisson's funeral ended shortly before 1 p.m. with a final cannon blast, and the crowd dispersed to their homes, for the public houses and restaurants remained shut until evening. Several mourners set off for a private meeting at the Exchange, and five or six directors of the Liverpool and Manchester Railway, among them Joseph Sandars and Charles Lawrence, travelled the two hundred yards up Rodney Street to the home of Henry Booth, so that they might discuss the extended running of next month's services – up from five trains a day to six – and consider whether it was at all possible for trains to carry enough water to ensure that a stop at Parkside was no longer necessary.

Huskisson as classical deity, originally over his tombstone in Liverpool,
now in London's Pimlico Gardens.

TWO DAYS LATER, at Byrom Street Chapel in the centre of Liverpool, Samuel Saunders rose for his weekly sermon. He had found a shadowy purpose in Huskisson's death. No one ever died in vain, he believed, especially in those days.

'Verily,' the Reverend surmised, 'every man at his best state is altogether vanity.' Those who gathered at the railway were a little too pleased with themselves, he said, and rather too sure of their exalted place in the world.

How little, amidst their mutual gratulations and social pleasures, did they suspect that there was among them a secret foe, who was sharpening his malignant eye on one of the most illustrious of their number, and was at that very moment drawing from his quiver the fatal shaft, which was not to be returned thither till, by its execution, it had filled the realm with consternation!

The clergyman had met Huskisson several times, and praised his work. Huskisson was the most efficient guardian of the empire's commercial interests; he was a political economist of the first order, and beloved by his constituents. But what happened to a man like this? 'This man, in the midst of all his honours, full of health and flushed with joy, and anticipating the greetings of thousands, is cut down in a moment, and now lies . . . in the mansions of the dead.'

There was a lesson to be learnt.

The enterprising inhabitants of this town should take warning lest, from their almost unprecedented prosperity, they . . . become vain and self-confident. A large community, succeeded in almost every venture, are in danger of losing sight of the hand of God, and of ascribing their prosperity to their own ingenuity, prudence and industry.

The people of Liverpool had brought the calamity on themselves, and there was not one reason but many. They dishonoured the Sabbath; they attended the racetracks; they drank, they swore, they resorted to prostitution, they let their young children run wild and villainous. Huskisson's death was not an accident, his congregation were told, but an 'awfully striking instance of Divine Sovereignty'. It was no coincidence that

he only, who identified himself with the interests of the town, and who was of more consequence to it than any other living man, should have been seized by the hand of death at such a moment, when taste and art had combined so assiduously . . . and when hilarity and rapture were expected to crown the day.

O N 27 September 1830, twelve days after Huskisson's death, Dr Thomas Weatherill wrote a letter to the *Lancet* from his surgery in Liverpool. He suggested that had it not been for bungled medical treatment, Huskisson would still be alive. The general opinion of his faculty, he claimed, was that the surgical advice he received had been 'unscientific, inefficient and imbecilic'. This was one way to ensure a little attention.

Dr Weatherill quoted a correspondent in the *North Briton* newspaper who was sure that a naval surgeon would almost certainly have amputated. In the *Liverpool Albion* he found another writer who backed up this assertion. Dr Weatherill concluded:

I am decidedly of the opinion that had prompt and energetic measures been undertaken the patient would have, in a great degree, been spared the torture of those spasms and twitchings of the muscles and tendons which are reported to have been so severe, and which proceeded from the loss of blood, and not, as has been stated, from the torn and mangled state of the nerves and other soft parts. Amputation, therefore, might have rescued the victim.

The doctor had spoken to eye-witnesses whose version of events differed from the official account. Huskisson bled profusely for a length of time, 'until his clothes and all about him were literally drenched in blood.' Dr Weatherill was astonished that even though all the great blood-vessels of the limb were entirely exposed, 'No means beyond placing a handkerchief round the leg were taken to stop the flow of blood; surely the haemorrhage might have been instantly arrested by securing those vessels.' Even if this were impossible, amputation should still have been attempted; and even if this failed to save Huskisson's life, he argued, 'no blame could be attached to any party.'

Two weeks later, one surgeon who was present at the accident drafted a reply. Dr William Whatton was plainly offended by the attack. Writing from his office in Manchester, he deigned to spell his assailant's name incorrectly. He wrote that he could not believe that the faculty of Liverpool was in general agreement with the doctor, or that they would act so irresponsibly as to pass judgement based on ignorance and gossip.

Mr Whatton stated that far from lacking naval or military expertise, the medical party attending Huskisson was full of it. Whatton himself was bred in the army, and learnt a great deal in the Peninsula Campaign, where he watched many of the leading military surgeons of the day. 'I can assure him that not one of them would have ventured upon an operation where the chances were so decidedly against its success.' The success rate of an amputation at that time, without either anaesthetic or antiseptic, and in a patient considerably more robust than Huskisson, was regarded as only 15 per cent.

The key factor was timing: it was essential to wait until the patient had recovered from the initial shock of the accident before amputation was attempted, 'and had shown at least some hope of outliving the operation.' Whatton then quoted extensively from the leading military surgeon George Guthrie, who had also served in the Peninsula and had written a guide so that others may benefit from his experience. In his lectures at St Bartholomew's, Dr William Lawrence had also referred to this manual. Guthrie advised that an operation should only proceed once a soldier's pulse became regular and his stomach easy, and not until he became less agitated and his general countenance revived. At this stage – which may occur as soon as two hours after the initial trauma – an amputation should succeed nine times out of ten. Dr Whatton reminded his detractor that Huskisson had still not reached this state even eight and a half hours after his accident; his pulse hardly improved; he became increasingly convulsive.

He quoted Guthrie to further his cause.

A cannon shot struck an officer in the middle of the upper half of the right thigh at the battle of Toulouse. He was carried into the house a short distance from the place of accident, and I saw him a few minutes afterwards; the soft parts were torn to the groin, the femur shattered to the trochanters, the femoral artery, vein, and anterior crural nerve, fairly divided. He was pale, ghastly, and little able to move; showed great anxiety of countenance; the pulse small and quick; the skin clammy; his face bedewed with a cold sweat; he could articulate but with difficulty, and did not appear to suffer much pain. Here any operation would have been instant death. As the fire of the enemy was very smart around the house, I remained in it with him and some other wounded, with the hope of being able to rouse him sufficiently with cordials and stimulants to bear an operation. He at first swallowed a little wine, but the constitution could not recover itself and in about two hours he was dead.

Dr Whatton found further support for delaying from another military specialist, Dr Hennen. He described a scene of devastation, with soldiers desperately wounded all around him. Their colleagues were demanding instant action to alleviate suffering, theirs and their friends'. But a surgeon 'will betray a miserable want of science indeed, if, in this crowd of sufferers, he indiscriminately amputate the weak, the terrified, the sinking . . .'

Mr Whatton informed Dr Weatherill that despite his assertions that only a handkerchief was used to stem the flow of blood, a ligature was also applied around the femoral artery as the very first act after the surgeons arrived at the vicarage. The Manchester man then questioned the competence of his Liverpool rival's own expertise by recalling Dr Weatherill's account in the *Lancet* two years before of his great difficulty performing an operation to remove a woman's cervix. Dr Weatherill had stated that if the same complications arose again he would have exercised no delay in removing additional portions of the abdomen to ensure success.

Such practice may consist very well with a member of a Salmagundi University or a graduate from Goose Creek; but no British surgeon, with the recovery of his patient and the fear of a coroner before his eyes, would dare to resort to such a measure.

He had some closing advice to Dr Weatherill's patients, 'if he has any, to pause before they again commit themselves to the chances of his scalpellum.'

Inevitably, Dr Weatherill replied two weeks later, the last of their correspondence. He maintained that even if an arterial ligature had been applied at Eccles, the delay was unforgivable, for by then the profuse haemorrhage was already abating, its fury having already defeated the strength of its victim.

There was another, newer tack: if Huskisson was able to amend his legal affairs, was he not also able to withstand an operation? 'I think he was, and so do others,' Dr Weatherill said. He reasoned that Huskisson's surgeons had nothing to lose, that it was better for a man to live with three limbs than to die with four, or indeed die with three in the presence of family members convinced that everything possible had been done to save him. 'Was every human mean employed to rescue the life of Mr Huskisson? I do most conscientiously, and most unequivocally, beg leave to say there was not.'

TWO WEEKS AFTER the events of September 15th, Liverpool returned to near-normality, although the town was forever changed by the railway.

The Siamese twins left Liverpool for London on the 26th, and they carried bruises. One Friday night a visitor named Smith had accused them of being 'imposters', suggesting they had never displayed the join at their midriff. The twins, still in their teens, were outraged by this claim, and said they would refuse to strip in public even if there were no ladies present. A scuffle ensued, in which one of the twins drew blood from Smith's nose, who then departed with talk of legal action. A few days later he withdrew this threat, and after reassurances from friends he conceded that the twins were not frauds after all. He did, however, believe that any future visitors should be warned about their violent tempers.

In the same week reports were received of the conquest of Mont Blanc by Captain Wilbraham of the Coldstream Guards. The peak had not been scaled since 1827, and the captain could find only six of forty local guides who would accompany him. Newspaper reports made special play of two facts: first, he had managed this feat without crampons; second, his descent had been perilous due to an excess of sun melting the snow, but he reached the ground without any hint of accident. The news was relayed to the Duke of Wellington in the Potteries, where he was visiting the porcelain factories of Josiah Spode and Josiah Wedgwood. It was his last official appearance before returning to Westminster, and he received a generally favourable reception, although the newspapermen were taking bets on whether he'd last the year.

At the foot of its political coverage, the *Liverpool Journal* had a generous offer for its subscribers: any reader presenting themselves to the newspaper office could pick up a free portrait of Huskisson, 'the finest specimen of lithography ever executed in Liverpool'. Two separate pictures were available, one full-face and the other in

195

profile, as just one printing plate would have worn out before demand could be satisfied.

Readers of other newspapers had to make do with poetry. An anonymous verse appeared in the *Albion*, with the rhythm suggestive of greased pistons:

> To celebrate national science and worth,
> Festivity crowning his will,
> Thus, fearless of danger, he kindly went forth,
> To patronise talent and skill.

> The wave of the hand and the smile of the eye
> We ne'er shall encounter again;
> To the kind recognition, in passing us by,
> We turn in remembrance and pain.

The *Liverpool Courier* rallied with a few lines from J D Newland of Chichester:

> Thy name, as thy talents, shall flourish immortal,
> Though scorn may detract, and though envy may frown;
> The temple of fame hath reopened its portal,
> And Canning invites thee to share his renown.

> Yes! England shall own, while in grief she repines thee,
> The force of thy genius and virtue combined;
> And truth shall inscribe on the tomb that enshrines thee,
> The Friend of His Country – The Friend of Mankind!

On 5 October, the *Liverpool Times* carried five notices on its front page regarding new railway companies. The directors of the Leicester and Swannington railway were keen to receive tenders for the excavation of a mile-long tunnel near Glenfield. The London and Birmingham railway announced that it had agreed a merger with the London, Coventry and Birmingham railway, and had applied to Parliament for an act to build its grand scheme. The Manchester and Leeds railway

The railway as figure of fun and terror, from 1833.

committee announced its intention to conduct surveys for a route that would link not only these towns, but also Selby, Rochdale, Todmorden, Bradford, Halifax, Dewsbury and Wakefield, and in so doing 'establish a complete line of Rail-road across the country'. The Liverpool and Chester railway announced the formation of its provisional committee, and a capital share issue of £200,000. The Liverpool and Leeds railway requested that any potential subscribers make their intentions known by 15 October to Sir John Tobin.

The directors of the Liverpool and Manchester announced that there would soon be special trips on the carriages occupied by the Duke of Wellington and his friends on the opening day, and that a new timetable was to be put in place. First-class trains would leave Liverpool each day at 7 a.m., 10 a.m., 1 p.m. and 4.30 p.m. (Sundays 7 a.m. and 4.30 p.m.), with second-class departing at 8 a.m. and 2 p.m. (Sundays 6.30 a.m. and 4 p.m.). In addition, a new protocol was now in force:

No fee or gratuity is allowed to be taken by any porter, guard, engine-man, or other servant of the Company, and the Directors are determined to enforce this regulation by the immediate dismissal of any person in their employ offending against it.

Previously, some staff had guaranteed better seats in return for better tips; the railways presented generous opportunities for all manner of new scams and minor corruptions.

The first goods train began travelling on 4 December 1830, when the Planet pulled eighteen wagons containing 135 bags and bales of American cotton, 63 sacks of oatmeal, 200 barrels of flour and 34 sacks of malt, a total load, including oil-cloths, of 75 tons. The journey took a little under three hours with several stops, but speed was not the issue that day, for the directors believed they had little left to prove. A few days before, the same engine, this time unladen, had made the journey from Liverpool to Manchester in under an hour.

Inevitably, Huskisson's accident was the first of many on this line. On 7 December 1830, when the Meteor and several carriages left Liverpool in the dark at 4.30 p.m. it was proceeded by a pilot engine – a new safety measure to ensure any obstructions were encountered ahead of passengers or freight, comparable perhaps to *The Times* correspondent's 'feelers'. But by the time it reached the Rainhill crossing it had advanced too far ahead, so that when it passed workmen on the line the Meteor was still imperceptible. The workmen only saw the engine once they had dragged a wagon halfway across the line, where they abandoned it in fear. A lantern was waved to alert the coming train, but the Meteor was going at 20 miles an hour. The driver switched the gear, and the guards in the carriages applied their new brakes, but the collision crushed the wagon to splinters. The engine and the first carriage were thrown off the rails, but there were no serious injuries. A broken engine wheel necessitated a long delay, but the carriages finally reached their destination with the aid of the nearest available auxiliary engine, which was the Rocket.

ONE YEAR AND ONE WEEK after its opening, the directors of the Liverpool and Manchester Railway reported on its performance in the six months between 1 January and 30 June. In this period, there had been 188,726 passengers, paying an average fare of 4s 7d and yielding an income of £43,600. Thirty-five thousand, eight hundred tons of goods had been conveyed between the towns, providing an income of £22,000. The Bridgewater Canal had been forced to cut its cotton haulage prices from 15 shillings per ton to 10. The directors concluded that their 'great experiment' had worked magnificently, and no mention was made of the uncertainty, just a few years before, of the importance of passenger traffic to its success. The report closed with a flourish: 'The Directors are happy to be able to state, that although nearly half a million passengers have been carried, only one fatal accident has occurred, and that arose solely from the perverseness of the individual sufferer.' That is to say, William Huskisson had already been reduced to a blip.

Epilogue

O N 15 September 2001, I took what I imagined would be a familiar journey. It was a windy but warm Saturday, and short trains from Liverpool to Manchester left several times an hour – two scornful, overheated carriages bowling themselves through Merseyrail stations painted yellow and grey. There is no class distinction on these journeys anymore, no Weekend First, no glamour, no diversions, no tables, no food, no cattle, no smoking. It's a shyly provincial insignificant line now, a trifling slither in the 20,000 miles of British rails.

I boarded the train: the doors still opened outwards. Someone in the carriage cleared his throat as a skateboarder put his feet up. As we pulled away, no one flung their big black hat in the air, or anywhere. It was the 10.19 stopping train to Manchester Victoria, a journey of 56 minutes, and although some trains shave a quarter of an hour off this, only the slow one gets all the stations: Wavertree Technology Park, Broad Green, Roby, Huyton, Whiston, Rainhill, Lea Green, St Helens Junction, Earlestown, Newton-le-Willows, Patricroft, Eccles – which isn't bad for £6 return.

The long tunnel out of Liverpool has a new beginning, with Lime Street Station opening in 1836 to handle the steady increase in traffic. The walls have been made safe since the original navvies first took their tools to them, but they have not been made attractive. The brown rock has ridges and troughs resembling a turmoiled sea. It is impossible to look at these carvings without feeling they were made with extreme physical endeavour and pain.

Even away from the tunnel the walls stay high until the open land flattens out after Broad Green. The stations have slippery, metal-mesh seats that repel both graffiti and extended stays. Many passengers on the outward journey are heading towards shops at the Trafford Centre or Everton versus Liverpool on Sky Sports One. At Earlestown the station backs onto a disused art deco cinema, which has since become a snooker hall, and which is now disused again. At its doors, a labrador ate someone's dropped food.

Past the canal near Newton the train picks up speed, crosses the M6, and runs past the GUS consumer goods warehouse. A few hundred yards from Newton-le-Willows on the outward journey, on the right hand side, stands the Huskisson Memorial, erected near the spot where he was struck, but raised up on the bank so that passengers of today may read of the horror and draw breath. Except they can't, because Parkside Station has disappeared, the intake of water neither a necessity nor a memory, and now even the slowest train rushes past, providing only the blurriest glimpse of a rectangular white structure resembling a railworker's rain shelter. The marble slab at its centre reads:

This Tablet,
   A tribute of personal respect and affection, has been placed here to mark the spot where, on the 15th of September 1830 at the opening of the railroad THE RIGHT HON. WILLIAM HUSKISSON M.P. singled out by an inscrutable Providence from the midst of the distinguished multitude that surrounded him, in the full pride of his talents and perfection of his usefulness met with the accident that occasioned his death, which deprived England of an illustrious Statesman and Liverpool of its honoured Representative, which changed a moment of noblest exultation and triumph that science and genius had ever achieved into one of desolation and mourning, and striking terror into the hearts of assembled thousands, brought home to every bosom for the forgotten truth that –
   'In the midst of life, we are in Death'

   The memorial was damaged some years ago by vandals and then left to disintegrate, but has since been restored. It can now be appreciated only if the train is delayed by a signal ahead, or if you slide down the bank on foot, a treacherous journey.

On 15 September 1890, precisely sixty years after this line opened, John White, a signalman with six years' experience, heard a terrible noise just beyond his signalbox at Gourock, on the banks of the Clyde. Gourock, a station that had opened just a year before on the Caledonian Railway, was expecting the 8.46 a.m. passenger train from Glasgow, twenty-six miles away, and White had just lowered his signals when the train jumped its rails at the station crossing and drove its first three carriages onto another track and towards an earthy bankside. The engine stayed on its wheels, but the tender ended on its side. The carriages remained upright, which explained why only three passengers reported injuries.

'I observed the train as it approached and passed the cabin,' John White told a board of enquiry one month later. 'And I noticed nothing unusually fast about its speed.' White remembered hearing the automatic brakes being applied about 120 yards from his cabin, but thought they were released again soon after. Anything else? 'The train had been telegraphed as passing Port Glasgow goods cabin at 9.15 a.m. – a minute late.'

The enquiry also heard from the driver, the fireman, the guard and the inspector of permanent-way, and concluded that the train was simply going too fast: the speed limit on entering Gourock station was 5 miles per hour. The driver claimed he may have been doing six, but the Board of Trade, which had taken over all responsibility for railway management and railway accidents, decided that the speed must have been considerably more. It also noted that 'there is no reason to suppose that this accident was due to any defect in the permanent-way,' with the same relieved emphasis that Huskisson's inquest had reached sixty years before. Inspectors of equipment still like nothing as much as human error.

I read this report as we sped towards Eccles. It was contained in a seventy-two-page foolscap document printed for Her Majesty's Stationery Office in 1891, priced at 7d. It was in a very delicate state, its crisp pages leaving brown flakes on my clothes whenever I turned a page. It cost me £36 at auction, which a few years ago I would have considered absurd, but now I had begun to regard as reasonable (I was prepared to go to £50). Railwayana is big business, and each week there are fairs and auctions to satisfy every extreme demand.

Whenever I went to these things I found I had to battle my way past an eager crowd of pensionable men with uncommon hair partings and the whiff of heartbreak about them, as if they'd been spending too long in airless rooms with their timetable collections and had begun to question whether they'd been wasting their weekends. Their aim was completion, but their task was impossible: there was now just too much railway stuff out there. They were a knowledgeable bunch, and the thing they knew most about was each other. At every trestle table you could hear, 'Hello Charles, got anything for me?' By which they meant, 'Got any new Severn & Wye Joint Railway routing labels?' or 'Got any more photographs of fish-train mishaps at Duddington pre-June 1959?' Auction prices for certain items were clearly out of control. In December 2001, the loco nameplate 'Knight of the Golden Fleece' was sold for £30,200.

These events would take place at The Model Railway Club behind King's Cross, at Myers Grove School in Sheffield, at St Leonard's Hall in Stafford, or at any other venue where stalls of tickets and timetables and share certificates and maps could be laid out economically. The first rule I learnt was, whatever you don't want to buy will be dirt-cheap, and the one thing you need to take home will be the costliest thing on the stall. The second rule was, any official report of a railway accident will be highly sought after, and normally unaffordable. Why this should be intrigued me, and I had a few explanations. An accident report may help us avoid the same fate in the future (possible but unlikely, as many of these reports were a century old and concerned exploding boilers). Or it could be because they are elegantly and exactly written (which they certainly are), and contain rare observations unobtainable elsewhere (our Gourock signalman, for example, noted that he arrived at his post at 4.30 a.m., and had forty-six different signals to control). But I came to conclude that, above all else, everyone just loves a good gawp.

In the space of a year I picked up five things of interest. I bought a small signed letter from Huskisson from 1806 detailing a problem he was having with an estate agent over whether or not fixtures and fittings were included in the sale of a house (irrelevant, but I wanted his signature, £20). I bought an empty envelope that Huskisson had signed and sent through the free parliamentary post to Davies Gilbert MP (the same man who had helped Richard Trevithick design his early steam engines, which I considered poignant and affordable at £6). The signatures were almost identical, although in the second the W was slightly more slanted. The envelope was stamped with Huskisson's red wax seal, which featured an elephant's head on top of a shield and the motto 'secura quies', short for 'At secura quies, et nescia fallere vita', which works out as 'But quiet slumbers and a life innocent of deceit'.

One item I bought and enjoyed made me think I was turning into an obsessive. An LP entitled *Trains In the Night*, on the Argo label, was pressed up in 1962 after a man named Peter Handford went out with a reel-to-reel tape-recorder to the Lickey Incline at Bromsgrove, and set his ear to the wind. His sleeve notes indicate what he got. As well as Lickey he also went to Steele Road Station on the Carlisle – Hawick – Edinburgh line, and at dawn one day a V2 engine, number 60927,

crosses the small road bridge, staggers slightly in an effort to keep a grip on the rails, then slips violently, belching steam and smoke, but with expert handling recovers and pulls strongly, if slightly more slowly, away, taking the heavy train round the curve towards Riccarton as the echoes of the exhaust beat mingle with the sounds of the early morning birds.

Stephenson and Sandars unleashed this dramatic and handsome world on us, and the world of the fanatic who tried to tape it for posterity. The steam music has gone, of course, but so has the use of Riccarton Junction. Other records in this series include *West of Exeter* and *Trains in Trouble*, in which engines struggle desperately in snow and fog, and the listener is rewarded with the unmistakable sound of drivers shouting a lot.

I also got a bronze medal, designed by S Clint and issued in 1830 to commemorate Huskisson's life and death (on one side was a profile of the statesman in relief, and on the other the inscription 'The successful vindicator of his own enlightened system of commercial policy. He lived to triumph over prejudice and to found a lasting fame.' £18). And I bid keenly for that accident dossier, if only to see if anyone else had been knocked down in similar fashion to Huskisson.

They hadn't, or at least not in the nine months ending 30 September 1890 covered by the report. Instead, passengers and staff had found many other grim and spectacular ways of injuring themselves on the railways. In these nine months there had been 773 deaths and 3,186 injuries, which was 3 deaths and 331 injuries fewer than in the preceding nine months. Decrease or not, this was still a lot of disaster. There were almost three railway deaths each day.

There were 67 collisions involving passenger trains, 36 cases of passenger trains jumping the rails, 10 cases of trains running into stations or sidings at too high a speed, 84 cases of trains running over cattle, 2 blown-up engines, 187 failures of axles and 482 failures of wheel tyres, almost all of them made of iron but a few made from new steel. The accidents happened all over the country with no pattern or lesson. The most one could learn from these events was how treacherous travelling by rail could be, and how far the railways had extended. Sixty years after the beginning, on the Great Eastern line, an incoming passenger train left the rail at facing-points at Fenchurch Street. On the Great Southern and Western Railway of Ireland, a passenger train collided with a goods train at Limerick. At Cardiff station on the Great Western there was a collision with a Taff Vale passenger carriage. On the London and South-Western, a light engine ran into the back of a goods train, the debris hitting a Midland excursion train. On the Manchester and Milford line, a locomotive boiler exploded at Maesycrugiau. And on the Lancashire and Yorkshire Railway a passenger train ran into some empty carriages by the buffers at Liverpool Exchange.

In addition to the railway accidents involving trains, there had been a lot of accidents in which people fell over bags on platforms or were injured while unloading wagons. And then there were fifty-six suicides.

B Y 1832, about 3,000 miles of track had been commissioned, by 1840 there were 1,775 miles, and by 1850 there were 6,200, mostly built by private investment. In 1844, the year J M W Turner first exhibited his masterpiece *Rain, Steam and Speed* at the Royal Academy (depicting an oncoming train on a Brunel bridge over the Thames), the great Railway Act attempted to instill some universal safety measures and financial solidity, and ensure that the system would benefit not just the capitalist entrepreneur 'Railway King' George Hudson, but also the third-class passenger. In short, it enabled mass social mobility at a penny a mile.

By 1846, at the height of the railway boom, Liverpool's pioneers had been proved right: the world in which they had first set upon with wide-eyed schemes less than twenty years before had changed beyond measure. From west to east, and from north to south, the

Liverpool and Manchester
RAIL-WAY.

TIME OF DEPARTURE

BOTH

From Liverpool & Manchester.

FIRST CLASS, FARE 5s.

Seven o'Clock Morning.
Ten „ Do.
One „ Afternoon.
Half-past Four Do.

SECOND CLASS, FARE 3s. 6d.

Eight o'Clock Morning.
Half-past Two Afternoon.

⁎₃⁎ For the convenience of Merchants and others, the First Class evening train of Carriages does not leave Manchester on *Tuesdays* and *Saturdays* until *Half-past Five o'Clock.*

The journey is usually accomplished by the First Class Carriages under two hours.

In addition to the above trains it is intended shortly to add three or four more departures daily.

The Company have commenced carrying GOODS of all kinds on the Rail-way.

January, 1831.

Four months after the opening, the journey is reduced to under two hours.

mechanical principle, the philosophy of the nineteenth century, spread and extended itself. There were 272 railway acts in that year. By 1846, in Wordsworth's accusatory phrase, no nook of English ground was secure from rash assault: the world had received a new impulse, and the railways became a metaphor for the Victorian age. Booth, Pease, Sandars and the Stephensons lived to see much of what they prophesied, and much beyond their imagining: the movement of people and ideas . . . capitalism unbound . . . the heroic boom in the iron and coal trades . . . the standardisation of time . . . the birth of the conservation movement . . . the expansion of the seaside . . . the spread of the commuterbelt . . . the poetry of Night Mail . . . the waiting at Crewe.

Overseas, almost all the early railways relied on British engines and expertise; conceived in the interests of trade, railways themselves became the great British export. On 18 February 1832, the *American Rail-Road Journal*, published from Wall Street, reported on the Liverpool and Manchester line as if Fanny Kemble was still aboard – 'It actually made one giddy to look at it, and filled thousands with lively fear'. The *Journal* was full of exciting destinations: a train track was running alongside the Erie and Hudson Canal, and new routes were planned for Kentucky, Tennessee and North Carolina. After the Civil War, trains opened up the interior and settled the West, to the extent that, less than fifty years after its birth, the railway had already acquired a golden age, a romance and nostalgia for the days before Westinghouse air brakes. In 1874, Lyman Abbott wrote in *Harper's New Monthly Magazine* of how George Stephenson toured every yard of the Liverpool – Manchester line on horseback 'after getting his breakfast of oatmeal with his own hands . . .' Abbott noted how things had changed:

The traveler going West steps to the ticket office of the Pennsylvania, the Erie or the New York Central Railroad. He purchases his ticket for San

Francisco. He gives his trunk to a baggage-master, gets for it a little piece of metal, and sees and cares for it no more. A porter shows him his place in the Pullman car. For six days and six nights he is rolled swiftly across the continent. Engineers and conductors change. He is passed along from one railroad corporation to another. At night his seat becomes a bed . . . He traverses broad plains, he passes over immense viaducts, whirls swiftly over mountain torrents on iron bridges, climbs or pierces mountains, but he never leaves his parlour; if need be, meals are brought to him where he sits . . . He is set down at the station in San Francisco. He looks at the clock in the station room, compares it with the timetable in his hand, and finds that his journey has been accomplished with all the regularity and punctuality of the sun.

It seemed a very simple business. He even got his luggage back.

The fastest Liverpool – Manchester journey today takes about forty minutes, but the Liverpool Chamber of Commerce has considered a Lightning Express Railway which would cut the time to eighteen minutes. The idea was proposed by a private company led by F B Behr, who argued that a monorail, already popular in Ireland, Belgium and France, would be just the thing for the home of inter-city railways.

'Gentlemen,' he ventured. 'You will agree with me that it is in the interest of both Liverpool and Manchester to have the most rapid and the safest possible means of personal communication with each other.' This was already beginning to sound familiar.

The enormous progress of civilisation . . . is principally due to the many inventions resulting in one form or another in increased facility for men to communicate with each other. But the more the means of communicating thought have been perfected the more eager became the desire to increase the facility and rapidity of personal locomotion, so as to bring both means of communication more in harmony with each other. That this is a want felt more and more everyday is testified by the large sums spent in all sorts of trials to increase the speed of express passenger trains . . .

Behr ran through various speed trials undertaken in France, Belgium and the United States, concluding that none of them were feasible without huge cost or risk to life. But now he believed he had an electric solution, and considered it ideally suited to run between the two cities where commercial steam passenger travel began.

There are no other two towns of such magnitude and joint interests so near together, and therefore they are really the first towns in the world which should profit by this new means of locomotion to a greater extent than any other two towns I could select . . . There are practically few difficulties. The gradients are especially suitable for attaining a very high speed with a moderate expenditure of electricity. The only expensive and difficult points in the proposal are the entrance into Liverpool and the supplying of electricity to any part of the line at the proposed tension of 700 volts . . .

He estimated the cost of construction to be £1.4 million. He proposed a total of 132 trains in both directions. Each train would accommodate sixty-four passengers, with annual ticket receipts of £200,000. There was no allowance at this time for freight traffic, partly because the delicate carriage balance of a monorail required that loads had to be distributed evenly on each side. On one monorail, the Listowel and Ballybunion in County Kerry, a piano was once balanced by a cow. On the return journey the cow was balanced by two calves. The calves were returned with one on each side.

The eighteen-minute monorail journey between Liverpool and Manchester has yet to happen. The money could not be found; there were serious concerns over safety. This was in 1898.

THE DEATH OF WILLIAM HUSKISSON is now just the famous first in an accident enthusiast's list of notable disasters, where it is the only one to involve just one casualty. All the others are vivid in their huge toll or spectacular crushing of iron and steel.

The people I met at the railway fairs knew the details as if they had just rushed from the scene: 60 dead in a single-line crash at Camp Hill, Pennsylvania in 1856, after which the driver at fault took his own life; 23 killed at the Clayton Tunnel crash on the London – Brighton line in 1861; 33 dead in the Abergele collision on the Chester – Holyhead line in 1868; the collapse of the Tay Bridge, the longest in the world, in a storm of December 1879, killing everyone aboard an afternoon train for Dundee – about 80 in all; the Armagh collision of 1889 in which many children on a Sunday school excursion were among the 78 dead, an accident that led the Regulation of Railways Act later that year to make automatic vacuum brakes compulsory on all passenger trains; the collision at Kentwood, Louisiana, in 1903 in which one train on the Illinois Central railroad ran into the back of another, killing 32; the catastrophic Quintinshill disaster of 1915, in which a troop train on its way to Liverpool was involved in a multiple pile-up, killing at least 227 (though the exact numbers were never known).

Many less sensational incidents had occurred on the Liverpool and Manchester Railway in the years immediately following Huskisson's demise. They involved new locomotives, derailed and mis-shunted and runaway: the Goliath, the Etna, the Mars, the Liverpool, the Bee, the Ajax, the Titan, and the Firefly, involved in at least thirty minor accidents in the years to 1835, each pursued by a director's investigation, each apparently unable to prevent the next. The first fatality since Huskisson occurred in the early morning fog of 23 November 1832. A delayed service from Manchester was loading luggage at Rainhill when the following train, the Fury, failed to spot it in time (passenger demand now dictated that trains ran as often as once an hour). The Fury was fitted with a new but primitive brake, but its operation was hampered by greasy rails. A soldier on his way to Ireland lost his life in the crash, and a new regulation was issued soon after: staff on any delayed train should forego their usual ticket-collecting and other duties and charge back up the line with flags and lanterns to warn the next arrival. Other accidents – passengers leaning out of the doors, stepping from a carriage with the train in motion – confirmed the need for public education; it took a while after Huskisson's death for the public to value the advice of experts.

The Rocket was employed on the Liverpool and Manchester railway until the mid-1830s, although it seldom conveyed passengers after 1831 and was used mainly for engineering duties. The railway directors' minutes show it was sold to James Thompson on behalf of the Earl of Carlisle for £296 in 1836, who ran it on the Midgeholme colliery line until 1844. Between 1851 and 1862 it was locked away at Stephenson and Co's Newcastle factory, after which it was finally recognised as a piece of significant restorable engineering and was obtained for display at the Patent Office museum in London. It arrived on loan at the South Kensington Museum in 1876, and apart from a sojourn at the V & A and the National Railway Museum in York, has been exhibited near this site at the Science Museum to the present day.

B UT THE ROCKET on display in the twenty-first century is somewhat removed from the one that collided with Huskisson. Several shunting accidents in the 1830s necessitated replacement parts. A brake was fitted to the wheels. Elements of the locomotive were raised, lowered, scrapped, remade and generally improved upon throughout its working life, for no one considered the possibility of historical attraction (or the possibility that replica Rockets would one day be displayed at the Henry Ford Museum in Michigan and other sites in Baltimore, Kansas and Illinois). Despite its greatly diminished form, its rough iron hulk still generates thrills in those who see it. It has long been stripped of its yellow paint, and guards at the Science Museum don't mind if you touch the boiler or the spokes of its tremendous wooden wheels, believed to be the genuine thing from 1829, and for a moment you may close your eyes

The Rocket outside the Patent Office in 1876: much altered,
but saved from the scrapheap.

and imagine hurtling towards Parkside, the Rocket's scalding chimney showering tiny droplets of vapour on your cheeks. Even a cursory examination will reveal a nameplate showing that the Rocket is just called Rocket, and although the pronoun was used by Henry Booth and George Stephenson in the writings, it is now largely frowned upon by purists.

In 1923, Buster Keaton was putting together his early seven-reel film *Our Hospitality*, a caper set in the early 1830s about two feuding families in New York and the South, when he decided that an old train should take his character and his sweetheart (his real-life wife Natalie Talmadge) cross-country. The train he chose was not an old early American locomotive but the Rocket, because Keaton thought it looked funnier than any other piece of transport he had ever seen. A working reproduction was built in California in a few months, and is the noisiest star of the silent movie. Inside the carriage it pulls, Buster juggles his hats; outside, the Rocket is stoned by frightened locals.

Keaton knew an icon when he saw one. For all George Stephenson's future achievements – all the other lines to York, Buxton, Leeds and Leicester, all the surveys of railways in Norfolk, London and the Scottish borders – it was the impetus provided by the Rocket at Rainhill and the Liverpool and Manchester Railway that remains his greatest accomplishment. That and his standard track gauge, which triumphed over Brunel's competing 7-foot span used on the Great Western Railway; it is the one constant through a parade of steam, diesel and electric.

George Stephenson was the inspiration, although his son was the more productive engineer, at least in terms of miles laid. Everyone knows the Rocket, but his greatest achievement was in the surveyance and construction of new lines, and a skill for methodic management that he shared with his great friend Joseph Locke. Between them they were responsible for a complex programme of routes in Britain, France and Holland before and after the boom and bust of the 1840s. After five years of arduous construction, Stephenson completed the London and Birmingham line in 1838 (the first important route into the capital), but is otherwise best remembered for his tubular-plate railway bridges, including the Britannia Bridge over the Menai Straits that linked London to Holyhead and the Victoria Bridge in Montreal, once the longest bridge in the world. 'As I look back upon these stupendous undertakings,' he told some friends in Newcastle in 1850, 'it seems as though we had realized the fabled powers of the magician's wand.'

Joseph Locke was shaken by his role in Huskisson's death, although no official blame was ever laid at his door. He continued to drive locomotives into his old age, famously directing Napoleon III on a trip from London to Southampton (and then back again when the sea was judged too rough for sailing). In 1847 he became MP for Honiton, and held the seat until his death in 1860. He remains one of the great unsung railway engineers; when he died *The Times* contested that he completed the triumvirate of great British railway pioneers with George Stephenson and Brunel, but his reputation has waned for want of a persuasive biographer. The Grand Junction railway from Liverpool to Birmingham (1837), the London and Southampton line (1840) and the Lancaster and Carlisle Railway (1847) were among the most troublesome of the period, but Locke forced them through with ruthlessness and sound economic principles that ensured they made money for their investors. In 1855 he met with an accident that had a peculiar resonance. While surveying a new route in France with the contractor Thomas Brassey, the scaffolding on which they were standing collapsed and a beam fell across Locke's leg, causing a double fracture. Local doctors recommended amputation, but Locke resisted. He kept his leg, but walked with a heavy limp for the rest of his life.

In October 1846, at the height of railwaymania, Henry Booth wrote to Charles Lawrence from his home in Liverpool. After his stint as secretary and treasurer, Booth had served as general manager of his railway, and Lawrence had got together with several prominent directors of subsequent lines to pay tribute to his twenty-year dedication. Booth thanked him (and them) with some ardent observations of 'originating this great movement'. He recalled working for Joseph Sandars and his co-directors, who,

without favour from the Legislature, or encouragement from the public, while the risk was evident and the gain problematical, with intelligence, perseverance, and singleness of purpose, pursued their work till success crowned their labours, and multitudes were eager to follow in their steps.

Booth went on to become secretary of the Grand Junction Railway and the London and North Western line, and he took out patents on carriage couplings, lubricating grease for bearings, and a new locomotive furnace. He became one of Liverpool's borough magistrates, and concerned himself particularly with the problem of providing insurance and compensation to railway passengers in the event of accidents and injury.

Emily Huskisson did not remarry, and she lived a pious life at Eartham until her death in April 1856 (she is commemorated next to a statue of her husband in Chichester Cathedral). She kept her grief in check by commissioning a bound collection of Huskisson's speeches, and devoting herself to the perpetuation of his fame. Her estate was inherited principally by the grandson of her late sister Harriet, and at her death £5 was distributed 'to each poor widow in Eartham'. Her will also remembered the widow of Reverend Thomas Blackburne, who had helped make her husband comfortable in his final hours at their vicarage. There is no record of her ever returning to Liverpool, or ever travelling again by train.

Fanny Kemble played Lady Macbeth before leaving for the United States in 1832. She endured an unhappy marriage for the sake of her two daughters, but turned against her husband publicly in the 1840s after he inherited two slave plantations in Georgia; Kemble became one of the most eloquent voices in the abolitionist movement. She made the occasional return to England, reading Shakespeare in the provinces with a tear in her eye and a fat cheque in her purse, but her greatest success lay with her talent for writing. The journals of her youth, which included the account of riding with George Stephenson and Huskisson's accident, became bestsellers. She divorced her husband when her children were adults, and developed a great friendship with Henry James, who summed her up perfectly at her death in 1893: 'The great thing was . . . she had abundantly lived.'

Charles Vignoles died in 1875 after a distinguished career that outdid his rivals for both longevity and variety. He became president of the Institution of Civil Engineers, he served on the Royal Commission on the Ordnance Survey, and was a Fellow of the Royal Society and the Royal Astronomical Society. His greatest achievements lay outside England – the Tudela and Bilbao Railway, a suspension bridge at Kiev and the Dublin and Kingstown line (the first great railway in Ireland). His tracks were built predominantly to Stephenson's standard gauge, though he personally believed that one of 6 feet promised greater stability. His great-grandson, Keith Vignoles, has written that he deserves to be better remembered, but that he is unlucky that most of his creations have been either demolished or absorbed in grander schemes. Above all he was unlucky to have met as forceful a man as George Stephenson, and he regretted his lack of credit for the work he considered to be his greatest achievement of all.

Between bouts of serious illness and bankruptcy, Richard Trevithick spent the rest of his life designing an ill-fated tunnel under the Thames and a 1,000-foot public memorial to parliamentary reform, but his greatest success remained with fixed high-pressure steam, which drove Cornish corn threshers and pumping mechanics for the silver mines of Peru. Not long before his death he wrote to Davies Gilbert with indefatigable self-belief:

I have been branded with folly and madness for attempting what the world calls impossibilities . . . This so far has been my reward from the public; but should this be all I shall be satisfied by the great secret pleasure and laudable pride that I feel in my own breast from . . . bringing forwards new principles and new arrangements of boundless value to my country.

The Siamese twins Chang and Eng travelled from the King's Arms to great notoriety in the United States, where they continued to be exploited until settling down in North Carolina with their wives and twenty-two children.

The Adelphi was rebuilt and enlarged in 1912, and flourished as Liverpool's premier hotel for ocean-going passengers steaming to and from the New World. Its large Sefton Suite was a replica of the first-class smoking lounge on the Titanic.

Wellington's government lasted for precisely two months after the opening of the railway, his downfall hastened by his failure to accommodate what remained of the Canningites and to acknowledge even the possibility of parliamentary reform. He left office with the clamour of southern riots in his ears, and the admission that 'I am more afraid of terror than I am of anything else.' He avoided trains wherever he went, not taking one again until 1843, when he accompanied Queen Victoria on a journey on the London and South Western Railway, a line engineered by Joseph Locke. But he did see the huge railway expansion of the 1840s as an investment opportunity, and became reliant on George Hudson's advice regarding share issues.

The Reform Bill finally passed in 1832, and saw the removal of some rotten boroughs and the extension of the vote to a large sector of the male middle classes. Despite Huskisson's avowed opposition during his lifetime, many of his former colleagues came round to supporting it. It was very much an act of the new railway age, a modest democratic advance emerging alongside the improvement in social mobility and the increasingly powerful merchant class. The Bill won wide support in Liverpool, and was championed in Parliament by William Ewart MP, Huskisson's successor.

THERE ARE A FEW MEMORIALS to Huskisson's achievements scattered around the country, and the National Portrait Gallery has a noble painting by Richard Rothwell, but generally he is remembered as that man who got knocked over by that train at the opening of that railway. This is better than not being remembered at all, not least if it leads on to an understanding of the support he gave to the railway enterprise in Parliament, and his advocacy of civilising social reforms at a time when it would have been easier to do nothing at all. He was a champion of trade and the free movement of people, and he sincerely supported his constituencies. If every male politician becomes a statesman fifteen years after his funeral, Huskisson had a strong claim to the title when he was still alive.

Huskisson was the subject of a biography within a year of his death, and it was the sort we now understand as 'authorised' – approved of and cleansed by his widow and friends. Edward Leeves' *Memoir* is a poetic and classical account, and one that strives to elevate its subject above the clamour of political animosity that rose again not long after his funeral. The picture that emerges is of a man overflowing with intelligence and generosity. Several times Leeves mentions the complete lack of sarcasm in Huskisson's speeches, an omission regarded as the surest sign of the open mind. The one word that sums him up best – and it is ironic given his own physical frailties – is upstanding. Huskisson's most notable fictional appearance occured in George Eliot's *Middlemarch*, in which he is first referred to as a champion of mercantile interests, and then as a victim of progress. In the early 1830s, the waggish John Raffles undergoes a complex journey mid-way through the novel, first by stage-coach and then by a recently completed railway, 'observing to his fellow passengers that he considered it pretty well seasoned now it had done for Huskisson.'

It is not entirely ludicrous to wonder what would have become of him had he not stepped off the train. Would he have become Prime Minister? I doubt it. Even in an era of wild instability at Westminster, there was general agreement that his best chance had gone; he chose a career in Canning's shadow, and at his friend's death found that he was not equipped to emerge from behind it.

But he would likely have found a secure post in Peel's government, perhaps in the Home Office had his health allowed, shaping some pre-Gladstonian reforms. He was not one of our greatest nineteenth-century politicians, but he was an eminently valuable one: he served the future.

WE PULLED INTO MANCHESTER two minutes early, but this was at a time when railway companies, terrified of being fined and mad on bumping up those percentages in their passenger charters, produced timetables with delays built-in. So even if you're a little early, you're actually a little late; and if you're truly and expensively late according to the timetable, there is a modern ritual to perform: a wait of uncertain duration is announced by a uniformed soul sounding unnaturally positive, contractually apologetic and inevitably nasal; weary passengers take this as a cue to list the best excuses for delays they've ever heard – 'unexpected fish-stock on the line'; and then everyone on board speed-dials home with details of their precise location and a stoic determination to make it home against unenviable odds.

On the day I travelled, there were two significant pieces of rail news. One was really a story about immigration and refugees, concerning the many people who each week risked their lives trying to enter England by clinging onto the underside of trains speeding through the Channel Tunnel, and the other was the publication of the second volume of the Cullen Report. This was the official analysis of the Ladbroke Grove train accident of October 1999, in which thirty-one died in a head-on collision. It also touched on the accidents at Newton Junction, Watford South, Bexley, Newton Abbot, Southall and Norton Junction between 1991 and 1998. The Hatfield crash of October 2000, at which four men lost their lives at the crack of a rail, occurred after the enquiry opened, and was not part of its remit.

The report made several suggestions – the establishment of an independent accident investigation body; a more unified approach to safety under a new chief rail inspector – but it was not keen to apportion blame. It only hinted, for example, that a great many problems stemmed from the government White Paper of July 1992 entitled 'New Opportunities for the Railways'. This resulted, the following year, in the privatisation of the rail industry, and two opportunities in particular: a whacking potential profit for government and investors, and a new chance for the rail passenger to face interminable delays on trains and at stations that were no longer owned by the same company that owned the track. By 1997, the functions of British Rail had been divided up into 100 businesses and sold. A glossary at the back of the report provided a glimpse of what the railway had become: MOLA, OPRAF, RAIB, SPAD – master operating lease agreement, office of passenger rail franchising, railway accident investigation branch, signal passed at danger. Clearly, Liverpool's pioneers would not recognise these terms, but would they want to?

Three weeks later, Railtrack was placed into adminstration. The receivers were called in, its shares were suspended on the London Stock Exchange, its chief executive resigned, its shareholders braced themselves, and it was announced that Railtrack was to be turned into a not-for-profit organisation. In 1963 Sir Richard Beeching had become 'the most loathed man in Britain' for closing 5,000 miles of track and more than 2,000 stations, but now there were other candidates. The government announced that the rail industry was not being renationalised, but admitted that Railtrack had been a managerial disaster. Railtrack countered that the real culprits had been government transport officials. Amidst the chaos and catastrophes it was possible to forget that most journeys by train pass off without historic hitches. But following the Railtrack announcement, BBC news held vox-pop interviews at Liverpool Lime Street. One man complained that his daily journey was a nightmare.

Then a woman said the same thing. Then another man. An interviewer asked whether there hadn't always been terrible delays and ridiculous excuses even in the so-called golden days of British Rail. 'Yes,' one man said, 'But every month, now it's just got worse and worse and worse . . .'

The example of the Liverpool and Manchester Railway held a few distant warnings. The railway remained independent until 1845, but since 1831 had begun accepting the freight wagons of many different individuals and companies which leased the track on a monthly basis. This was a condition of its original parliamentary enabling act: in an attempt to limit profiteering, the owners and operators of the line would not be the sole operators of its traffic. In practical terms, this system proved shambolic, and created endless disputes over responsibility. Further confusion was caused by the addition of branch lines from Parkside to Wigan, Preston and Warrington, also managed independently of each other. In 1839, a parliamentary committee heard how engine drivers of different companies developed dangerous and unproductive rivalries. The former British rail signalman Adrian Vaughan described a familiar scenario in his history, *Railwaymen, Politics and Money*:

The many and varied machines with their individualistic drivers, owing allegiance to a variety of employers, plied to and fro without much regard for safety: collisions were common . . . When damage occurred there would then be a row between the various parties as to who was to blame and who was to pay.

I detected a familiar ring.

The truly strange thing is, the railway system in Britain today is not like it was sixty years ago, but what it was like 160 years ago. The little stations have gone in the interests of efficiency. The trains are controlled by a management structure that comes and goes with the tides and the promise of super shake-ups and super pay-offs. We have the big trunk lines left, the giant project routes between the cities where the money is made, and the rest is park-and-ride. We may justifiably ask how far we have travelled.

At the time of writing, a period of nervousness and extreme uncertainty in the railway industry, Railtrack survives as a managerial entity, but plans are well advanced for a takeover by Network Rail. Safety records are maintained by the Strategic Rail Authority, the Health and Safety Commission and the National Rail Safety Authority, whose staff calculated that in a twelve-month period between 1999 and 2000, 931 million separate journeys were made on British trains between 2,500 stations, resulting in 47 deaths (not including 274 suicides) and 2,768 injuries, a large increase on previous years.

In January 2002, the Strategic Rail Authority announced a new ten-year plan, and the Prime Minister said that of the £30 billion state funding in this period, the majority would be going on safety, not least on the replacement of worn track and new signalling measures; Tony Blair conceded that his government had no idea how much the rail network had been neglected until the Hatfield crash exposed the full picture. But some things will never change. There will always be very bad accidents, and very bad accidents will always necessitate a visit from the Transport Secretary in a dark coat, in a bid, presumably, to understand the horror of what has just occurred – and in an effort, one imagines, to ensure that an accident of this nature should never happen again. But there he is once more at Potters Bar in May 2002 with that long ashen face, flanked by nervous officials shaking their heads, surrounded by reporters announcing seven further railway deaths and considering how long it's been since they last told their readers and listeners and viewers the mind-curdling fact that, passenger by passenger, and mile by mile, the train was still the safest form of ground travel yet invented.

Huskisson's tomb in St James's Cemetery:
this is how we honour him today.

IN MID-SEPTEMBER 2001, I walked through St James's Cemetery. My vision of it had been formed by a description in Nathaniel Hawthorne's *Notebooks*, written in the years he spent in Liverpool as the American consul. On 14 September 1853 he wrote:

It is a very pretty place, dug out of the rock, having formerly, I believe, been a stone-quarry. It is now a deep and spacious valley, with graves and monuments on its level and grassy floor, through which run gravel-paths, and where grows luxuriant shrubbery. On one of the steep sides of the valley, hewn out of the rock, are tombs, rising in tiers, to the height of fifty feet or more; some of them cut directly into the rock with arched portals, and others built with stone. It was a warm and sunny day, and the cemetery really had a most agreeable aspect. The statue of Huskisson stands in the midst of the valley, in a kind of mausoleum, with a door of plate-glass, through which you look at the dead statesman's effigy.

You may not be surprised to learn that the plate-glass has gone. But John Gibson's fine marble effigy, a life-sized study of Huskisson robed like a Roman senator, has gone too. What's left is a rectangular tomb, but it is impossible to read its inscription: the glass has been replaced by coarse metal bars, prohibiting entrance into the mausoleum and creating a cold, stern impression to the passing visitor. The evident message is: you have no business here.

The cemetery as a whole remains atmospheric and affecting, lined on one side by those catacombs, and on the other by a wall of gravestones cowering beneath the gothic threat of the Anglican cathedral. Here lies Mary, daughter of James and Mary Ritson, who died 11th October, 1831, aged 6 months and 11 days. And Captain William Wildes, Born at Arney Town, State of New Jersey, US of A, 3rd July 1793, Died at Liverpool 4th March 1835. And John Jones, who died 28 March, 1838, aged 61 years after 34 hours severe suffering from injuries received by the falling of his horse.

Gravestones also lie flat around Huskisson's mausoleum, and some are covered with the debris of construction – wooden planks, sandbags, an orange road cone. But nobody was constructing anything: that crap had all been brought here for fun, and to serve as goalposts or skateboard ramps. The steel bars in front of the tomb are spaced a few inches apart, enough for people to lob drinks cans and newspapers and old swabs of clothing in there, rusting and rotting by Huskisson's side. Like most people interested in old trains and nineteenth-century history, I am an unreasonably sentimental man, and I was surprised I didn't cry when I saw this terrible scene. But I couldn't: too shocked to do anything else, I just gawped.

In September 1830, people had gathered to witness one story but departed with another, and at the time it was hard to judge which was the more significant – the birth or the death. In quick time, as the train girdled the world, Huskisson's life faded from view until he was just an alarming but winning anecdote. If he was remembered at all, his name often became Huskinson, because it sounds as though it ought to be that way. His accident continues to provide us with one of those big, charming metaphors of progress: it announced a new force in the world, and the Rocket became the ultimate symbol of the new machine; old men wandering across its path didn't have much of a chance.

What would Huskisson have thought of the railways today? He would have been astonished. The system he supported continues to be, with some exceptions, a thing of wonder. There is much dilapidation and malpractice; in particular, the country where the railways began has realised only recently that it has neglected its brilliant past. But there is also a way of crossing continents and seas by bullet trains and tilting trains, and a way of conversing and reflecting as the world shrinks beyond the window. The railway – and not just the warming nostalgia of steam – continues to give pleasure and practical satisfaction to a restless world. As we wait for late arrivals on draughty platforms, it is easy to forget Henry Booth's proclamation from the opening day: the world had received a new impulse, and everything would be different.

Sources and Acknowledgements

I have tried, wherever possible, to base this account on contemporaneous material. The Huskisson papers at the British Library (Add MSS 38734–38770) were the main source of his correspondence and speeches; the collection of journal cuttings and notes scattered throughout the volumes were also useful. The many newspaper reports of the building of the railway, the Rainhill Trials, and Huskisson's accident were invaluable, as were the full accounts in the periodicals. Industrial accidents are rarely witnessed by the diary-keeping classes, but I was fortunate that Huskisson's featured in so many, contradictory as they were. Henry Booth's inspiring history of the railway remains the principle insider's account, and his minutes from directors' meetings provide the most reliable report of the construction of the line.

A few books have been particularly good guides. Chief amongst these is Robert E Carlson's scholarly examination of the building of the railway (1969), which is still the definitive economic study of the project. The two prominent and very readable histories from the 150th anniversary by Frank Ferneyhough and R H G Thomas were also rich sources of pleasure and information, although in all accounts Huskisson's demise is glossed over with as much speed as the railway directors would have wished.

I would like to thank all those who have helped me with this book, especially the many librarians at the British Library manuscripts department, the London Library, the Liverpool Central Library, the Manchester Central Library, the Bodleian and the National Railway Museum in York. My thanks for material, advice and hospitality to Penny Wickham, Mark Cropper, Esther Freud,

David Morrissey, John Penney, Richard Weeks, Richard Coombes, John Adderley, John Sheffield, Peter Price, Julian Loose and all at Faber, and Pat Kavanagh and all at PFD. And all my love, as always, to Diane Samuels.

The images on pages 2, 34, 69, 88, 95, 124, 136, 139, 144, 155, 197 and 216 are reproduced with the kind permission of the National Railway Museum / Science & Society.

Journals

American Railroad Journal, New York, 18 February 1832
Annual Register, 1830, pp 144–148; 205–206, London, 1830
Blackwood's Edinburgh Magazine, Vol 28, pp 823–830, Edinburgh and London, 1830
Cornhill Magazine, Vol 35, pp 830–840, Smith, Elder & Co, London, 1913
Fraser's Magazine for Town and Country, Vol 2, No 9, pp 252–263, 1830
Gentleman's Magazine and Historical Chronicle, Vol 100, pp 263–265, London, 1830
Harper's New Monthly Magazine, pp 375–394, 1874
Lancet, Vol 2, pp 945–951, London, 1829–1830; Vol 1, pp 129–132, 1830–31
Mechanics' Magazine, Museum, Register, Journal and Gazette, Vol 14, M Salmon, London, September 1830
Monthly Review, Vol 15, pp 253–265, G Henderson, London, 1830
New Monthly Magazine and Literary Journal, Part III, pp 484–486, London, 1830
Newcomen Society Transactions, London, Vol 9, pp 78–93; Vol 10, p 120, Vol 11, 67–89; Vol 50, pp 109–138; Vol 52, 171–179; Vol 54, pp 55–77
Quarterly Review, Vol 42, pp 377–404, John Murray, London, 1830; Vol 45, pp 504–548, 1831; Vol 51, pp 358–359, 1834
Transport History, Vol 6, No 1, pp 30–52, London, 1973

Newspapers

Albion, 12, 19 October 1829; 23, 30 August, 6, 13, 20, 27 September, 4 October 1830
Liverpool Courier, 14 January, 11 March, 6 May, 29 July, 19, 26 August, 2, 30 September, 7, 14, 21 October 1929; 6, 13, 20, 27 January, 3, 10 February, 31 March, 12, 19 May, 14, 21 July, 4, 11, 25 August, 15, 22, 29 September, 6, 20, 27 October, 10 November, 8 December 1830

Liverpool Journal, 21 August, 18, 25 September, 2 October 1830
Liverpool Mercury, 10, 17, 24 September, 1 October 1830
Liverpool Times and Billinge's Advertiser, 15, 22 September, 13, 20, 27 October
    1829; 17, 24, 31 August, 7, 14, 21, 28 September, 5 October 1830
Manchester Courier and Lancashire General Advertiser, 14 August, 4, 11, 18
    September 1830
Morning Post, 17, 18, 20, 25 September 1830
Spectator, 18 September 1830
The Times, 16, 17, 18 September 1830

Books and Pamphlets

von Baader, Joseph Ritter, *Huskisson und die Eisenbahnen*, Munich, 1830
Bailey, Michaeal R and John P Glithero, *The Engineering and
    History of Rocket: A Survey Report*, National Railway Museum, York, 2000
Bamford, F and the Duke of Wellington (eds), *The Journal of Mrs Arbuthnot*,
    Macmillan and Co, London, 1950
Booth, Henry, *An Account of the Liverpool and Manchester Railway*, Frank Cass and
    Company London, 1830 (reprint 1969)
Booth, Henry, *Henry Booth: Inventor-Partner in The Rocket and the father of
    Railway Management*, Arthur H Stockwell, Devon, 1980
Brady, Alexander, *William Huskisson and Liberal Reform*, Oxford University
    Press/Humphrey Milford, London, 1928
Burton, Anthony, *The Rainhill Story*, BBC, London, 1980
Carlson, Robert E, *The Liverpool and Manchester Railway Project*, Augustus M
    Kelley, New York, 1969
Coleman, Terry, *The Railway Navvies*, Hutchinson, London, 1965
Lord Cullen, *The Ladbroke Grove Rail Enquiry, Part 2: Report*, HSE Books,
    Suffolk, 2001
Davies, Hunter, *George Stephenson, A Biographical Study of the Father of the
    Railways*, Quartet, London, 1977
Dendy Marshall, C F, *Centenary History of the Liverpool and Manchester
    Railway*, Locomotive Publishing, London, 1930
Devey, Joseph, *The Life of Joseph Locke*, Richard Bentley, London, 1862
Ellis, Hamilton, *British Railway History 1830–1876*, George Allen and Unwin,
    1954
Fay, C R, *Huskisson and His Age*, Longmans Green, London, 1951
Ferneyhough, Frank, *Liverpool and Manchester Railway*, Robert Hale, London,
    1980

Greville, Charles C F, *Memoirs*, Longmans, Green & Co, London, 1875

Huskisson, William, *The Speeches of the Right Honourable William Huskisson with a Biographical Memoir Supplied to the Editor from Authentic Sources* (Leeves) (3 vols), John Murray, London, 1831

Huskisson, William, *Speech on The Silk Manufacture*, J Hatchard & Son, London, 1826

Jack, Ian, *The 12:10 From Leeds* (in *Granta 73: Necessary Journeys*), London, 2001

Jennings, Humphrey, *Pandaemonium: The Coming of the Machine as Seen by Contemporary Observers*, Andre Deutsch, London, 1985

Kemble, Frances Ann, *Record of a Girlhood* (3 vols), Richard Bentley & Son, London, 1878

Lee, Charles E, *The Evolution of Railways*, Railway Gazette, London, 1937

Marshall, Dorothy, *Fanny Kemble*, Weidenfeld and Nicolson, London, 1977

Leeves, E, *Biographical Memoir of the Right Honourable William Huskisson*, Private printing, London, 1831

Maxwell, Sir Herbert (ed), *The Creevey Papers*, John Murray, London, 1905

Meville, Lewis (ed), *The Huskisson Papers*, Constable, London, 1930

Morgan, Bryan (ed), *The Railway-Lover's Companion*, Eyre and Spottiswoode, London, 1963

Nock, O S, *The Railway Engineers*, B T Batsford, London, 1955

Reed, Brian, *The Rocket: Loco Profile*, Profile Publications, Windsor, 1970

Rocket 150, Official Handbook of the 150th Anniversary of the Liverpool and Manchester Railway, British Rail, London, 1980

Rolt, L T C, *The Railway Revolution: George and Robert Stephenson*, St Martin's Press, New York, 1960

Ross, John A (ed), *Collected Papers Concerning Liverpool Medical History, Eighth British Congress on the History of Medicine*, Liverpool, 1977

Saunders, Samuel, *A Sermon Occasioned by the Death of the Late Right Hon William Huskisson*, D Marples, Liverpool, 1830

Semmens P W B and Goldfinch A J, *How Steam Locomotives Really Work*, Oxford University Press, Oxford, 2000

Simmons, Jack, *The Railway in England and Wales 1830–1914*, Leicester University Press, 1978

Singleton, David, *Liverpool and Manchester Railway: A Mile By Mile Guide to the World's First "Modern" Railway*, Dalesman Books, North Yorkshire, 1975

Skeat, W O, *George Stephenson: The Engineer and His Letters*, Institution of Mechanical Engineers, London, 1973

Smiles, Samuel, *George and Robert Stephenson*, Harper and Brothers, New York, 1868

Thomas, R H G, *The Liverpool and Manchester Railway*, B T Batsford, London, 1980

Various, *Remarks on the Comparative Merits of cast Metal and Malleable Iron Rail-ways; and An Account of the Stockton and Darlington Rail-way and the Liverpool and Manchester Rail-Way*, Charles Henry Cook, Newcastle, 1832

Various, *Returns of Accidents and Casualties as Reported to the Board of Trade by The Several Railway Companies in the United Kingdom During the Nine Months Ending 30th September 1890*, HMSO/ Eyre and Spottiswoode, London, 1891

Vaughan, Adrian, *Railwaymen, Politics and Money*, John Murray, London, 1997

Veitch, George S, *Huskisson and Liverpool*, Transactions of the Historic Society of Lancashire and Cheshire, 1929

Veitch, George S, *The Struggle for the Liverpool and Manchester Railway*, Daily Post Printers, Liverpool, 1930

Vignoles, Keith H, *Charles Blacker Vignoles: Romantic Engineer*, Cambridge University Press, Cambridge, 1982

Vignoles, Olinthus J, *Life of Charles Blacker Vignoles*, Longmans, Green and Co, London, 1889

Walker, Charles, *Joseph Locke*, Shire Publications, Buckinghamshire, 1975

Walker, James Scott, *An Accurate Description of the Liverpool and Manchester Railway*, J F Cannell, Liverpool, 1830

Webster, N W, *Joseph Locke: Railway Revolutionary*, George Allen and Unwin, London, 1970

Williamson, James A, *George and Robert Stephenson*, Adam and Charles Black, London, 1958

Index

Page references in *italics* are to illustrations